'Summer swung her _____
to wince as the strap _____
Her notecase, which _____ _____ unac-
countably to have sli_____ deeper in; it was probably her
mad progress down that path which had jolted it. She stood
the backpack down on the counter and pushed her hand
right inside it. No notecase. Suddenly apprehensive she
began to pile her things out on to the counter, then abruptly
remembered her loose-change purse in the pocket of her
cut-offs. She paid the man, muttering an explanation of
sorts, then hurried out of the shop into the sunlight once
more.

There was a bridge over the river which fed the lake. People
congregated here but right now it was deserted. Everyone
was either having a meal or booking themselves a room for
the night, she supposed.

Sitting on the sun-warmed grey stone, Summer turned out
her backpack down to the last paper tissue, then her
pockets.

Both were empty. Somehow, somewhere, she had lost her
notecase. Apart from three pound coins, some ten-pence
pieces and a few coppers, she was destitute in a foreign
land!'

Summer's holiday in the Lake District has begun disas-
trously. Her aunt has forgotten her and gone away, a violent
man has threatened her, and now her money has been lost.
Only attractive Felix Delgado can enable Summer to survive
her time in England – and only Felix can help to untangle
the web of mystery that is tightening round the village of
Castlebridge . . .

SUMMER IN THE LAKES
Judith Saxton

CORGI
F·R·E·E·W·A·Y

SUMMER IN THE LAKES

A CORGI FREEWAY BOOK   0 552 52456 5

Originally published in Great Britain by Corgi Freeway Books

PRINTING HISTORY
Corgi Freeway edition published 1988

This book is set in 11/12pt Paladium

Corgi Freeway Books are published by Transworld Publishers Ltd.,
61–63 Uxbridge Road, Ealing, London W5 5SA,
in Australia by Transworld Publishers (Australia) Pty. Ltd.,
15–23 Helles Avenue, Moorebank, NSW 2170, and in New
Zealand by Transworld Publishers (N.Z.) Ltd., Cnr. Moselle
and Waipareira Avenues, Henderson, Auckland.

Reproduced, printed and bound in Great Britain by
Hazell Watson & Viney Limited
Member of BPCC plc
Aylesbury, Bucks, England

1

'Here we are, miss. Virginia Cottage. Pretty, in't it?'

The cab driver got out of his vehicle, grabbed Summer's bulging backpack and carried it across the grass verge, then he stood it down to open the small wicket gate set in the quickthorn hedge.

Summer scrambled out of the cab as well and stood, blinking, in the hot noon sunshine. Her mother had made her pack lots of sweaters because she said it was a well-known fact that England was usually cold and wet, especially in summer. Much she knew! Summer had been in England a fortnight already and every day had been blue and gold. London had been a furnace and she had been glad when the history course had ended, fascinating though it had been. Life in a big city, sleeping twelve in a dormitory in the hostel each night and touring historic London by day, was tough by any standards and what with the heat and Summer's wretched shyness and youth – she was the youngest member of the history group by three long years – she had been happy to say her farewells to her fellow countrymen and set off for the station. An only child, she was simply not used to being surrounded by other people twenty-four hours a day, and was really looking forward to a quiet couple of weeks in the Lake District with her godmother, Aunt Peggy.

'You'll get some peace and quiet there, honey,' her mother had said as she added yet another sweater to the pile already in her daughter's suitcase. 'You'll like Peggy, she was good to your father and I when we were dating and, my word, that countryside sure is beautiful. As I remember, it's gentle country, soft, dreamy, as though it's been asleep for the past couple of centuries. A good place to wind down, get your breath, but not the kind of place where anything much actually happens.'

Now, following the cab driver down the path towards the cottage, Summer could only agree with her mother's words. It sure was beautiful but there did not seem to be another dwelling place for miles and the cottage looked not just sleepy but sleeping. Creeper overhung the windows and even trailed a lazy finger or two across the front door, whilst the silence was so profound that when the driver suddenly banged the knocker Summer could almost feel the cottage's stunned reproach at such a vulgar, twentieth-century noise.

'Anyone home?' Summer said after a moment, when no one came to answer the summons. 'It sure is quiet.'

'Aye. Mrs Catchpole's probably down t'garden,' the man remarked comfortably. 'We'll gi' her a moment.'

They gave her a moment and then the man knocked again, but once more no footsteps came hurrying. The noise just echoed and died away in the afternoon stillness.

'We'd best tek a look round the back,' the driver decided. 'Happen Mrs Catchpole's right down t'back, diggin' or summat.'

Summer followed him round the side of the cottage. She was glad she had not paid the man off and

6

assaulted the cottage alone. He was middle aged and fatherly in his saggy grey slipover and navy serge trousers, but reliable somehow. He was nothing like the New York cab drivers, Summer thought, remembering the wisecracking, fast-talking guy who had driven her from home to Idlewild Airport. He was not even much like the Cockney cabby who had brought her to the station that very morning. That man had been young and sharp-featured, with pin-up pictures all over the dashboard of his cab and a nice line in abuse for fellow road-users, not at all the sort of guy she would have felt comfortable with, searching for a missing godmother. But this cab driver was taking it for granted that he would hand her over to Mrs Catchpole or wait with her until someone turned up.

The path down the side of the cottage was narrow and overgrown by abundant currant bushes through which Summer and her companion had to thrust their way, but they emerged at last into the back yard, which proved to be much bigger and grander than the front of the cottage seemed to warrant. There was a wide terrace, a big lawn dotted with gnarled old trees, an orchard to one's right and wild garden to one's left and, across the bottom of the lawn, a vegetable plot simply teeming with greenery set in neat lines.

Summer stared and her heart sank doubtfully. There was no sign of a living soul here, and what was worse, there were other signs which seemed to point to Aunt Peggy being away for the day. There was a summerhouse, locked and barred, a swingseat with no cushions or canopy, and the cottage windows were sealed tight.

'Oh heck, she's out,' Summer said. The cab driver put the backpack down on the terrace steps and looked, as she had, from the swingseat to the summerhouse to the cottage itself. 'Guess I'll have to wait for a while, and I'm so thirsty! Is there a telephone near? Though I don't know who I'll call . . .'

The cab driver suddenly smote his head with the back of his hand. An idea had obviously struck him.

'Come back to t'cab wi' me for a mo, miss, and I'll radio back to base. I've got a feeling . . .'

He and Summer retraced their steps but Summer stayed in the front garden, examining the flowers, whilst the driver's voice murmured deeply and an answering voice quacked a shriller reply. Then he backed out of his cab and walked towards her, his face creased into a frown.

'I'm sorry to tell you, miss, that there's been a misunderstanding. Mrs Catchpole left for a week's stay in Scotland this morning! Told her driver she'd got to be back by the twelfth because she'd have a visitor then, all the way from the United States. That's you, I dessay?'

'I reckon. But . . . you say she's gone for a whole week?'

The driver nodded. For a moment they stared at one another, then Summer slung her pack back into the cab.

'Oh dear, what'll I do? Mom said Aunt Peggy was awful absentminded, and there was a muddle . . . I've been on a history course and the organizers changed the dates twice . . . I'll have to go back to London and give my mom a buzz. She'll tell me to go back home, I guess.'

Driving along the quiet country roads towards the station, the driver told Summer what he had suddenly remembered back there in the cottage garden.

'I were listening on the radio when t'call came through to go to Virginia Cottage first thing,' he

8

explained. 'I weren't near enough to go up for her, I just heard a station call. By 'eck, she's a nice woman, your Aunt Peggy. She'll be fair moithered to think she's missed you.'

'If only I knew someone else, I might stay with them, just for a week,' Summer said dolefully. New York in August would be so hot and dirty, and besides, it would spoil Mom's own holiday, though she would pretend she didn't mind. She had gone off to a colleague's holiday home by the shore, but she would not have been able to go had not the history course suggested itself.

'Why does it have to be someone you know?' the driver asked, steering his cab carefully round a blind corner. 'It's only a week, after all. Why not get yourself bed and breakfast in a cottage, wait out t'time? Ever been to t'Lakes before?'

'Well, no. This is my first time over.'

'There you are, then! Hundreds of youngsters go bed and breakfasting here in August; all you need are casual clothes and strong legs! You can climb the hills or swim and boat on t'water . . . You'll love it, I dessay, they all seems to.' He paused delicately. 'Unless you're short, like? Though it's not pricey, bed and breakfast.'

'No, that'ud be all right, I guess.' Summer considered the idea, which she was beginning to find increasingly attractive. She had plenty of money, both her parents had seen to that. She had scarcely spent a cent of her London allowance and Mom had given her money for Mrs Catchpole which, in the circumstances, she would feel no qualms over spending on bed and breakfast. In fact the more she thought about it, the more the idea of a week on her own appealed to her. It was beautiful here, but what was more important was that if she stayed alone and

9

managed, how pleased her father would be! He and her mother had separated and then divorced years ago, but they were still on amicable terms and Summer spent quite a lot of time with Pop and his new wife, Louisa. Pop had paid for the history trip partly because he wanted her to mix more and partly because he longed for his child to see the Lake District. When he had been a boy living in Manchester all his happiest holidays had been spent in the Lakes. He had hiked here, climbed, swum, boated. He admired the sturdy independence of the people and their forthrightness and wanted her to know them, too.

Mom would worry, of course, that went without saying. She worried about everything Summer did and a good few things Summer would never have dreamed of doing. But this time she need know nothing about it until it was over. Summer imagined herself rushing across the arrivals lounge at the airport and telling Mom all about it. 'I've had a great time, though I didn't meet Aunt Peggy because she'd got her dates mixed up, but it didn't matter, I stayed bed and breakfast for a week by myself. All right? Mom, of course I was, I'm sixteen years old! I met some great guys . . . one of them was real nice. Perhaps I'll write to him . . . I said if he ever came to New York . . .'

Mom would be pleased because she thought all girls Summer's age should be interested in boys. What was more, all boys ought to be interested in her daughter, and that was the part which disappointed her about Summer. Other girls had dates by the score; all Summer had were A grades and hobbies!

'Well, love, what's it to be?' The cabby slewed round in his seat and asked the question she had been asking herself. 'The station, or someone doing bed and breakfast?'

Summer looked out of the window as the cab

slowed. They were passing through a village. White-washed cottages with their thatch so old that it sagged over the bedroom windows like unruly hair, stone-built buildings with tiles cushioned with moss, gardens bright with old-fashioned flowers. There was a village green and a pond with geese on it and nearby a clump of oak trees which might, Summer supposed, have stood in that selfsame spot when the first Elizabeth was on the throne. It was an awe-inspiring thought for a history student.

'I'll stay – for a while, at any rate,' Summer said breathlessly. 'Not right here, I guess, somewhere with a diner, where I can get a meal. What'll I do first?'

The cabby slowed even further, almost stopping his car whilst he considered her question. Summer thought of him as the nearest thing to a friend she had in England and he obviously took his responsibilities seriously.

'Well, love, if you'll tek my advice you'll get yourself some dinner fust go off,' he announced. 'And then mek your way to Castlebridge. I'll drive you to a decent caff and point the way from there; it's easy enow. You tek the road to the first stile, go over it and up into t'hills . . . beautiful country, it is . . . and after you've gone no more'n a mile or three you'll see Castlebridge and the lake below you and from there it's all plain sailing.' He chuckled. 'Even if you missed t'village you couldn't miss t'hikers, there's 'undreds of 'em, boats for hire, little beaches for swimming, ideal for 'olidaying. Aye, that's my advice, lass – head for Castlebridge!'

2

Summer, with her heavy backpack chafing her shoulders, had a good meal in the village cafe her friendly driver pointed out and then set off along the road, his words ringing in her ears. *Take the first proper footpath on the left, it's beautiful walking and it'll lead you, gradual-like, down into Castlebridge in time for your tea. Get yourself booked in first, though; happen there'll be competition for beds after five o'clock.*

She obeyed the instructions and very soon discovered that she had far too many clothes on for slogging up a hillside in the hot sun. Denims, a blue-and-white checkered shirt and sneakers were just not right for a country walk. Summer found a convenient patch of shade beneath a tree, sat down and shed her backpack, her shirt and her denims. She fished some cut-offs out and slid them over her pants, then changed her bra for her bikini top. She felt much better, particularly when she took off the barrette which had held her hair off her face and tied it into a pony-tail well clear of her neck so that any breeze around could caress her skin.

This, she realized later, had been a mistake, though she did not know it for some time. She was too busy admiring the breathtaking views as she climbed and also in congratulating herself on deciding to take the cab driver's advice. If she walked, stopped for the night, then walked again, she would see a great deal of this beautiful countryside and would feel she had made good use of her time in England.

After an hour, however, she began to feel her shoulders and the back of her neck tingling ominously. At first she ignored the warnings. She would be all right, she was used to the hot sunshine of a New York summer and this English sun would not burn like that, surely? But soon common sense prevailed and, with a sigh, she stopped again. Her tender, gold-freckled neck could be a mass of blisters and peeling skin by evening if she did not take care. She put her long-sleeved shirt back on and loosed her hair so that it screened the back of her neck. Then she slung her backpack – wincingly – over one shoulder, promised herself some After-Sun as soon as she reached civilization, and set off once more up the side of a very steep hill.

Her second mistake came in climbing with such grim determination that, as it transpired, she missed the path. She was plodding and dreaming, the ground going beneath her feet at a satisfactory rate, when she realized that she was on short grass, with sandy patches and stones, but with no sign of a path.

A few weeks ago, such a discovery would have made Summer miserable; she would have worried. But now, almost without her noticing it, Summer's self-reliance was improving in just the way her father had hoped when he had urged her to go on the history trip. It was annoying that she was off the path, but by no means a disaster. In fact it might well prove a good thing, since she was far nearer the summit of this particular hill than the path would have led her – she could see it now she was looking, far below

13

her, a white wiggle on the green – so now was her chance to check up and see how much further she had to go to reach the lake and Castlebridge.

Resolutely, with her backpack now swinging from one hand since its close association with her stinging shoulder had proved too painful, Summer climbed on. And got her reward. She reached a small plateau, with boulders, a cliff-face and a few spindly rowan trees, and was able, for the first time, to see how far she had travelled and how much distance lay between her and her objective.

Below her, brilliantly blue, was the lake, and beside it a village which she supposed must be Castlebridge. She could see a bridge, anyway, and a river and houses. She walked nearer the edge and told herself that she could be down there, if she trotted, in ten or fifteen minutes. She glanced at her watch, which said four-twenty, and then swung round again to have a look at the climb to the summit. Was it worth going right up there, just so that she could say she'd reached the very top? But this was no spot for climbing, or not without proper equipment, anyway. The cliff here was absolutely sheer; she would have to find some other road to the summit, and she did want to get to Castlebridge before there was too much competition for lodgings!

She was about to continue across the plateau so that she could descend from the other side, when something caught her eye. Was it a cave? Caves had always fascinated her and promptly she decided to explore. Not very far, because of the time, but it would not hurt just to peep!

Summer wondered, afterwards, why she had gone round the big boulder at the mouth of the cave so quietly, almost as if she *knew* she was spying on someone. When she popped her head round the edge

14

of the boulder and looked eagerly towards the cave, the man, bent over an opened rucksack, did not even look up.

Startled, in fact shocked by his presence, Summer stayed absolutely still for a second, and in that second she saw, in a muddled sort of way, that the man was playing with cards, or some sort of game. He had a box by his side and the cards laid out, only they had pictures on them, tiny scene, and he was picking a card up, tapping it, doing something to it . . . Summer moved a fraction, so eager was she to see just what was happening.

At her movement the man looked up. For a split second, the two stared at each other. Summer saw a short, thickset man with black hair, a five-o'clock shadow on a brutal-looking chin, and dark, narrowing eyes. He was clad in a singlet and faded pants and he wore black sneakers, one of which was fastened with string instead of a lace. He reminded Summer of Caliban in *The Tempest*, a play she had recently seen performed at the Old Vic.

He was not a pleasant sight and Summer stepped back, a little startled by his expression. Seconds later she was glad she had, for the man uttered a growl and launched himself across the small space which separated them.

'What the hell . . .? You dirty, spying little . . .'

Summer did not wait for him to finish the sentence; she simply turned and fled downhill, running raggedly, and knew all too soon that the man was following her. She glanced back and saw him bounding bow-leggedly but fast over the rough ground, his expression, even at a distance, still furious and vengeful.

All Summer's common sense should have been telling her to stop and face the man, ask him what the fuss was about, but intuition or native wit or perhaps just plain old cowardice simply told her to keep running, and boy, she obeyed! She fairly sizzled down the side of the hill, slithering, tripping, catching her clothing on branch and bramble, until she shot round a corner thickly planted with trees and bushes, doubled back on herself and crouched, panting and dishevelled, under an extremely prickly gorse bush.

She now saw that she was barely twenty yards from the path and down that path, chattering blithely, were coming a small group of youngsters. There were two girls and four boys, all lighthearted, but sufficient, it seemed, to stop Caliban in his tracks. Summer heard her pursuer slither to a halt quite near her, saw his legs remain still for a moment, obviously undecided, and then begin, almost reluctantly it seemed, to climb the hill down which he had just come with such speed and energy.

The young people came on. Summer hesitated, agonizingly torn over the most sensible course of action. If she got up and walked down the path behind them, in full view of Caliban, would he descend the hill again and catch up with her? Not that he could do much with all those people within call, but she was sure from his demeanour that he was not the sort of man to trifle with, though when she considered, what harm had she been doing? She had been walking in the hills as so many others were doubtless doing, she had crossed no fences, climbed no walls, so she could not possibly have been trespassing. She had been dumb to run because he shouted – she should have stopped and asked him what was the matter, faced up to him!

But even now she felt uneasy over the thought of doing any such thing. He had sounded so furious, the expression on his face had been so unpleasant, that she was glad she had simply got going. Cautiously, still half crouching, Summer began to rise, casting a hunted look up at the hillside behind her. There was no sign of Caliban. Indeed, had it not been for the faint cloud of dust her precipitate descent and his hot pursuit had called into being, a cloud which still hovered, she might have believed she had imagined it all. Far above her though, she thought she saw a flicker of movement, and that decided her. A braver person would have gone back up the hill, secretly, to see just what Caliban thought he was up to on that high and lonely plateau but, Summer decided, flicking a strand of hair wet with perspiration off her neck, she was not that sort of person. She would go quietly down the track behind the group of hikers, find herself somewhere to stay and try to forget all about that perfectly horrible guy.

Resolutely she rejoined the path she had left earlier and sauntered down the hillside. As she went she settled her backpack on her shoulder and a twinge of pain reminded her that she really must get something for sunburn before she did anything else. A few days spent miserably in a darkened room suffering from sunburn was no recipe for a good time!

'Can I help you?'

Summer had been browsing in the chemist shop whilst other customers took tubes of toothpaste, sun-oil and soap over to the counter, but now she realized she was being addressed. By a tall, grey-haired man with a handsome face, what was more. He was smiling at her. He looked, Summer thought, like one of those distinguished film-stars of the seventies . . . clean-cut, that was the word. He sounded like one, as well, like James Mason or Laurence Olivier. Which was, of course, why she stammered.

17

'I h-hope so! I've caught the sun real bad; do you have anything for sunburn?'

The man turned to a shelf behind him, took down a bottle, shook it, and held it out to her.

'This is a special concoction of my own which is very efficacious. If you don't mind my mentioning it, with that glorious hair you should always take the sun in small doses, but I think if you keep your neck and shoulders covered, and spread this lotion on three or four times a day, you'll have no more trouble. Keep out of direct sunlight until the skin's cool to the touch and take aspirin for the pain . . . Do you have any aspirin?'

'No, but it isn't painful. I th-think I caught it in time,' Summer said, taking the bottle. 'How much do I owe you?'

The chemist named a sum and Summer swung her backpack off her shoulder, trying not to wince as the strap scraped her skin, and delved inside it. Her notecase, which had been right on top, seemed unaccountably to have slipped deeper in; it was probably her mad progress down that path which had jolted it. She stood the backpack down on the counter and pushed her hand right inside it. No notecase. Suddenly apprehensive she began to pile her things out on to the counter, then abruptly remembered her loose-change purse in the pocket of her cut-offs. She paid the man, muttering an explanation of sorts, then hurried out of the shop into the sunlight once more.

There was a bridge over the river which fed the lake. People congregated here but right now it was deserted. Everyone was either having a meal or booking themselves a room for the night, she supposed.

Sitting on the sun-warmed grey stone, Summer

turned out her backpack down to the last paper tissue, then her pockets.

Both were empty. Somehow, somewhere, she had lost her notecase. Apart from three pound coins, some ten-pence pieces and a few coppers, she was destitute in a foreign land!

For a moment the enormity of what had happened was so great that all Summer could do was to stare down into the rippling water beneath the bridge, willing herself not to cry, not to panic, not to run screaming down the street. Her passport was safe, she had her clothing and bits and pieces, it was simply her money which had gone. All she had to do was get in touch with the folks back home, explain, and wait for a money order to arrive.

Only what would she do whilst she waited? She could call America collect as she had planned to do earlier in the day, but there would be a lapse of some time before the money could reach her, possibly quite a long lapse. Her mother was staying with friends at the shore, so it might take a while to contact her.

She remembered her mother's many contingency plans: if things go wrong, go to the American *Consel*, she had urged. In the Lake District? Perhaps it would be best to go to the cops and ask if they could lend her some money until her panic was over.

Sitting there, sternly ordering her tears to quit making her look a fool and a wimp, Summer thought back, and had little doubt at which point the notecase had been jerked out of her backpack. It had been when she was flying down the hillside to escape from Caliban, of course. Which was a good reason not to go straight to the police, because she could imagine all too well what they would say.

'Go back over the ground you covered and have a good look for your notecase,' a well-meaning cop would advise. 'If you can't see it, come back to us.'

It was of course the sensible thing to do, but Summer felt a good deal of reluctance to go back. Caliban would have to come down from the hills eventually, as she had done. The thought of meeting him up there, as dusk crept down, sent shivers along her spine.

Once she was calm again, Summer scooped everything back into her backpack, blew her nose, and stood up. The chemist shop was in a line of converted cottages and next door to it was a gift shop, adjoining that a cafe. She would go into the cafe, get herself a cup of coffee and a sandwich with her dwindling resources, and then decide what to do. After all, if she could find somewhere to spend the night she could return to the hillside very early next morning, before anyone, even Caliban, was about, and possibly find her notecase. That would be best, because then she would not have to cable for help or face the authorities.

Summer made for the gift shop since the entrance to the cafe was through the shop. She would have gone straight through without a glance around her but it was too crowded and a patient queue of would-be customers stood waiting. There was a notice over the counter asking people with rucksacks or big bags to leave them with the staff rather than block up the passageways between the tables, so she handed her backpack to a cross-looking girl lounging behind the counter chewing gum, and joined the queue. She was prepared for a lengthy wait but she was lucky.

'Anyone alone? Place for one free. You, miss . . . there you are, over there . . . See?'

The waitress, in jeans, T-shirt and a frilly apron, led her to the empty chair and Summer sank gratefully into it. She ordered coffee and a cheese-and-tomato sandwich and then leaned back and surveyed through her lashes the person sitting opposite her at the small table for two.

He was a young man; dark-haired, sallow-skinned, dark-eyed. He was drinking tea or coffee, she could not tell which, and he had a paperback novel propped up in front of him, giving her a good chance to stare. He looked rather nice, steady and dependable. He was not cute, as her classmates would have said, but his hair curled a bit, not much but enough to make the frame round his face more interesting, Summer thought. She wondered how old he was. Twenty? Twenty-two? She had no idea really, but thought he looked older than most of the people on the history course and they, by and large, had been in their late teens. Only, of course, people with thin faces and tanned skins did sometimes look older than they really were.

Summer wondered how old she looked. She was fair-skinned, with dark red hair (Glorious, indeed, she sniffed in retrospect at the chemist's words; auburn was glorious, or a rich raven black, not something between the two!) and, of course, a great many freckles. Freckles, she knew, made you look younger. Lemon juice helped to fade them, if you could be bothered. She had never tried it, though she had thought about it once or twice when she had been alone and horribly bored in the apartment.

A waitress approached, carrying a cup of coffee which had slopped into the saucer and looked as pale as Summer had felt when she had first missed her notecase, but at least it was hot and wet. She thanked the girl, gulped down a mouthful and gasped with relief as it slid down her dry throat. The young man smiled as she took another scalding sip and pushed the sugar basin towards her.

21

'Don't hurry it, it's hot, if not strong! D'you take sugar?'

The voice was deep, pleasant, the accent unmistakable. Summer felt her smile spread into an ear-to-ear grin.

'I can't believe it! You're American!'

The young man raised a dark eyebrow. Summer felt a swoon coming on; of all the boys in junior high, her favourite was Max Burnheim. He and he alone could raise one eyebrow in that particular fashion. Not that he ever noticed Summer Campion, he was far too busy dancing attendance on Billy-Jean Piensciew, who was so beautiful that even the teachers tried to date her. But the young man was speaking. Summer dragged herself out of her swoon to listen, and anyway, with both his eyebrows normally positioned again, she found herself quite capable of coherent thought.

'That's right, all the way from Oregon. You from Stateside? They've got an accent here which fools me sometimes – Shropshire, I think it's called.'

'Yup, I'm from New York.' Summer nodded so vigorously that a thick hank of hair fell forward, obscuring her view. She pushed it back behind her ear and looked hopefully at her fellow countryman. 'Gee, am I glad to meet you! I've lost all my money, my notecase has gone. What'll I do?'

'Hell, that is bad luck. Lost, was it? Or stolen?'

'Oh, lost, I'm sure. I ran down . . . Well, I better start at the beginning.'

Halfway through the rather involved narrative it crossed Summer's mind that she was actually talking to a stranger. She stopped short, her mouth dropping open and then closing firmly. She was the shy one who never spoke to guys, the one whose report cards were often spoilt by recommendations that she study less and play more. She felt warmth creep into her cheeks; he must think her awful, pushy and loud-mouthed.

'Go on! So you left your godmother's place in the cab, then set off to walk here . . . You still haven't got to the bit where you lost your notecase. If you know where you lost it you can go back and take a look. If you're not sure, put a notice in a shop window. If you're lucky it'll be handed in by nightfall.'

The boy's face did not look at all critical as he spoke, he just looked interested. Summer took courage.

'It's not that simple.' Summer took another invigorating drink of her coffee and suddenly – disappointingly – her cup was empty. She sighed and looked round for the waitress who was supposed to be bringing her sandwich, but the only one on view was taking a big order from a table crammed with hikers and did not look as though she would ever glance towards them. Summer pushed the cup away from her and started talking again. 'I walked all right, only I missed the path and found myself up right near the top of the hill, on a little plateau with a fantastic view. Then I thought I saw a cave so I went round the side of a big boulder and there was a guy there, spreading out cards, only they weren't ordinary cards, all over a flat-topped rock. He saw me and yelled . . . I ran, he sounded real mean. He chased me for miles, then I hid in some bushes until a crowd of folks came along and I tagged on behind them. I could hear him going up the hill again. I don't think he saw me.'

'And that's all? Sweetie, that guy probably saw your notecase drop and was chasing you to hand it over. Didn't that occur to you?'

'Well, no.' Summer hesitated. It sounded as

23

though it might have been possible and of course it could not possibly have occurred to her at the time as she had no idea she had lost her notecase. But she could still remember her pursuer's expression; he had been angry, the language he had used had been angry. She tried to explain to her companion.

'You're right, it didn't occur to me, but I'm sure it wasn't like that at all. He called me names . . . a dirty, spying little something-or-other . . . his face was all twisted and furious. I wondered if I was trespassing but I didn't cross any fences or walls or anything.'

'And you don't much want to go back and face a furious guy who might tell you off for trespassing?' The young man shook his head sadly, but he was smiling. 'Believe it or not, I can understand that. Oh, by the way, I'm Felix Delgado. Who are you?'

'Gee, how rude I am. I'm sorry! I'm Summer Campion. So what'll I do, Felix? I could just get back to London, I suppose, and find the airport and go back home. I've still got my ticket and my passport.'

This time, Felix raised both brows, which Summer found quite easy to resist. He looked like a teacher and a cross one at that. He looked like Mr Abrahams just before he made one of his scorching comments about Summer's poor performance in his P.E. class.

'Go home? With a godmother wanting to be your hostess for a fortnight, and with this weather? Summer, this is an opportunity which you may never have again and you'd be real dumb to turn it down! Get a job, use your skills . . . I'm sure you've got plenty . . . and enjoy your time here! Come to that . . .' His hand shot out as a waitress tried to hurry past. 'Sandy, honey, could we have two more coffees? And what's happened to my friend's cheese sandwich?'

'Sorry, Felix, we're rushed off our feet. Nell had a row with the boss and she's left, so we're one short.'

The waitress was a skinny little blonde with a lot of eye makeup, very pale skin and a warm and friendly smile which she turned on Summer. 'Sorry, miss. I'll go and get your order now. Shan't be a tick.'

The girl hurried off and Felix turned a triumphant face to Summer. 'There, you see? Do you think you could do a job like that? Nell lived in, same as most of the girls do, so if you got the job here that would solve two of your problems. As for your notecase, I'll come with you when I'm not working and we can look for it together, or do you think your muscular friend would knock me cold as soon as look at me?'

'Would you really – come with me, I mean? That'ud be neat!' Words, Summer found, could not express her relief but she tried a big smile, adding, 'Do you think they'd let me work here? I'd like to have a try, just till my money turns up. I got a Saturday job once, in the local diner, only Mom didn't want me to take it so I gave up the idea.'

The brow rose again. Slowly and, Summer thought, very sexily. Her stomach did a slow somersault.

'You gave it up because your mom didn't like the idea? What a good little girl you must have been!'

Summer knew she was being teased but, to her astonishment, she liked it. At home, she hated being teased. It was odd, yet Felix's teasing was quite different, and she realized it was because he had used the past tense – what a good little girl you must have *been*, not what a good little girl you are. He realized that she was no longer a good little girl, that she was quite capable now of making up her own mind and taking her own decisions.

'Yes, well. I'm an only child and Mom worries a lot. Besides, it was years ago.' Summer smiled without self-consciousness when he laughed. He had very nice teeth, strong and white. 'What do I do next, then? Go up to a waitress and ask if she's got any work for me?'

He laughed again, but shook his head.

'No, not the waitress, we'll ask to speak to the proprietor. If Nell really has left, then I imagine he'll leap at the chance of finding a replacement so quickly.'

'Right.' Summer stood up. 'I'll go now, shall I? Then I'll come back and drink my coffee when it arrives.'

'Sure, if that's the way you prefer to do it.'

To Summer's great relief, Felix stood up as well. He tipped his chair forward, did the same to Summer's, and then headed for the back of the cafe where a long counter separated the customers from the staff. As they approached it a waitress came out through a swing door which led, Summer could see, to the kitchens. She was carrying a tray with two plates of french fries on it and two empty cups. She slapped the tray briskly down on the counter, picked up the first cup, and proceeded to fill it at the coffee machine. She was quite a young girl, with rather a lot of spots, greasy dark-brown hair pulled carelessly back from a round, cheerful face, and glasses perched on the end of a turned-up nose. She smiled briefly at them both and, as soon as the cups were filled, turned back towards them.

'Want your bill, Felix?'

'Not yet, Liz, we've not had our order in full yet. No, I was wondering whether the boss is anywhere around.'

'Mr Bloxham? Anything wrong?'

'Not really. Could you give him a shout?'

Liz shrugged, picked up her tray and then backed into the door, butting it open with a plump hip. She

26

shouted through the opening, then let the door crash closed and headed, tray in hand, for the cafe once more.

Almost before the door had stopped swinging a middle-aged man with mean, close-together eyes and a down-turned mouth appeared behind the counter. He glanced briefly at Summer and then at Felix.

'Yes? What can I do for you?'

Felix put his hand on Summer's shoulder and she bounded forward, almost cannoning into the counter as she did so. She had forgotten her sunburn until that moment and Felix, who knew nothing about it, looked startled.

'Oh . . . Mr Bloxham . . . I hear you may want a waitress. Is that right?'

It was a simple enough question but the man's grey eyes hardened and he actually stepped back a pace as though he, too, had been touched on his sunburn.

'What makes you say that?'

Summer, having made her first bid for a job, was too surprised to answer but Felix did so for her. He said quietly: 'You look pretty busy to us and Sandy said you were a waitress short since Nell had left. Summer's at a loose end and needs some money so we thought . . .'

'Yes, Nell's gone, I was forgetting.' Mr Bloxham actually smiled at Summer, though the smile did not reach his shiny little eyes. 'Yes, I was going to put an advert in the window this evening . . . You know about rates and so on? We pay catering rates of course, not too marvellous, but we provide free board and lodging and we don't ask you to work for more than twenty hours a week, or not on the books at any rate.' He winked, a reptilian flicker of one thick eyelid. 'You interested? When can you start?'

'Umm . . . tomorrow?' Summer found herself

devoutly hoping that her notecase would turn up sooner rather than later; this was not a charming man! 'I don't . . . I haven't had time to . . .'

'Can she move in tonight, she means,' Felix explained as Summer's voice sank to an embarrassed mutter. 'Most places will be booked and if she's coming tomorrow to work . . .'

'Aye, she can go up about seven, when Beryl's had a chance to clear Nell's mess up. She took her stuff, of course, but there's no end of muck we'll have to throw out.' He looked directly at Summer and addressed her instead of talking to Felix. 'Be in the kitchen by nine tonight. You can start serving breakfasts tomorrow morning.'

Summer said that would suit her fine, the proprietor nodded and turned away, and Summer drifted back to their table in a daze. She had a job! She was going to be a working girl for a week or so. Mom would be horrified but she was not around to make Summer doubt her own abilities. Pop would be pleased. His second wife, Louisa, a self-reliant young woman Summer still felt guilty over liking, would be pleased as well. They'd kid her, of course, but they'd admire her for doing a job.

'We'll pop down to the cop-shop presently,' Felix said as he sat down opposite her again. He had lingered by the counter to pick up two more coffees and Summer's cheese sandwich and now he put the tray down on the table, pushed a cup over to Summer, and picked up his own. 'We may not hear news of your notecase, but at least it can be put on record as having been lost.' He raised his coffee cup. 'Here's hoping!'

Summer's heart, which had begun to sink over the prospect of visiting the police station, took a turn for the better. He was not planning to abandon her to her

28

own devices yet, then, he would go with her to the police. Summer chatted lightheartedly whilst they finished their meal, then strolled along beside him as they went through the village, listening as he pointed out his lodgings, the garage where he worked on a shift system – he had explained he was a student at Hatfield Poly, doing a holiday job – and other places which he deemed were of interest. By the time they reached the police station, Summer felt she was really getting to know Felix, and he her, and she entered the small, stuffy building with a light heart and a pleasant feeling of anticipation.

However, they drew a blank; no notecase had been handed in. And once this had been established and a description of the case taken down by the desk sergeant, Felix had to hurry off to his garage for a four-hour shift, leaving Summer to make her way back to the cafe alone.

Despite the proprietor's optimistic remarks, Summer found herself serving in the cafe and working hard, too, when she arrived there. By the time she went up two long and narrow flights of stairs and entered the little attic room, she was too tired to care that the sheets were probably the very ones Nell had slept in the night before. But as she fell into bed she was conscious of a good deal of satisfaction. She had enjoyed the work, the other waitresses were friendly and intrigued by her accent, the customers were the same, and when they sat down to their own meal it was a good one, the food well cooked and generously served.

Summer hunched the covers up over her shoulders and hastily pushed them down again. Despite a liberal anointing with the chemist's lotion her skin still throbbed and burned. What a day it had been, she mused, as the cool night air caressed her hot flesh. And whatever would Mom say if she could see her one-and-only, curled up in someone else's bed in someone else's sheets and thinking, not of her far-off homeland or the apartment or her fussy, over-protective mother, but of a thin-faced, dark-haired guy called Felix, who actually seemed to enjoy her company!

And then there was Pop . . . and Louisa. Pop would grin all over his face if he could see her now, and tell everyone that he'd always known she was a spunky one, with more to her than met the eye. He'd maybe even call her a chip off the old block and his favourite girl!

Summer was smiling as she fell asleep.

3

A cockerel, crowing its head off, woke Summer just as the sky in the east was staining with rose. She lifted her head muzzily from the pillow and looked around her. Of course, she was in the attic above the cafe, sleeping in Nell's bed. One of the other girls had referred to it as the dormitory but it was not as bad as that; it was a small room with a sloping ceiling partitioned off from the rest by plasterboard walls, but at least it was a room of her own.

It was quite decent too, Summer thought, seeing it properly for the first time. There was no carpet but the lino was cheerfully red and the furniture, though sparse, was clean. A white-painted chest of drawers with a mirror on top, a chair with a squashy red cushion and a range of hooks along the wall with a checked curtain pulled across were the sum total of fittings apart from the bed, but the walls were painted a pale yellow which made the room look sunny even when, as now, the sun had not actually put in an appearance.

Having approved of the room, Summer sat up on her elbow and tried to look out at the view, but all she could see was the colour of the sky, so she swung her legs out of bed and took a couple of steps across the floor, then pressed her nose against the window-pane. She had an excellent view straight out, but the window was the sash sort and open at the top, so she reversed it – top shut, bottom open – and leaned out, her fingers spreading over the warm red roof tiles. Down below her was the road and the bridge she had sat on whilst searching for her notecase and beyond that the lake, already streaking with the colours of the sunrise. If she looked sideways she could see what might well be the slate roof of Felix's lodgings and, by leaning out, the end pump at the filling station where he worked.

Hanging out of the window and smelling the freshness of the morning, Summer decided she could not possibly stay indoors. The lake was getting bluer as the sun rose, it was going to be another perfect day. She would go out right now, before she started work in the cafe, and see just what sort of a place this village was.

It did not take her long to dress since cut-offs and a boob-tube would suffice. It was too early to worry about the sun on her shoulders. She stole down the stairs, which creaked plaintively as if warning the rest of the staff that someone was about, and across the empty kitchen. It was curtained and dim, smelling pleasantly of food, but to her annoyance the door leading into the cafe was locked. She rattled the handle, then abandoned it and went over to the back door. She did not know where it led since she had not used it the previous evening, but it must have access to the outer world, she supposed.

It was bolted, but the bolts slid back easily and the key turned sweetly in the lock. Summer opened it and found herself in a wide delivery yard with a five-barred gate on her right leading on to a narrow alley which, she supposed, would run down to the main village street.

A city girl, she hesitated to go out and leave the

back door unlocked and the kitchen a prey to any passing stranger. Still, she could scarcely go off with the key and since she might want to get back indoors before the rest of the staff were up she could hardly lock it and post the key back through the letterbox. She hesitated, torn between desire and duty. Perhaps she should return to her room, but sleep was impossible with the cockerel still shouting his head off and the sun shining straight in, and besides, she did want to explore. She decided to risk a prowler; it was so quiet out here that she must surely be the only person in the whole world awake – or at least, the only person in the sleepy Lake District!

Summer crossed the yard, went out through the gate, down the alley and out on to the street. A glance was sufficient to show that the village was indeed deserted. Skeins of mist as insubstantial as smoke hung over the river, and the sun, edging enquiringly over the shoulder of the humped hill ahead, looked down on a scene of such peace and beauty that intruders, burglary or even a spot of trespass seemed as unlikely as men from Mars.

I won't go far though, Summer decided, walking towards the lake with the hire boats drawn up on its margin. I'll keep my eye on the cafe and if anyone looks like walking round the back I'll go straight over there. But it seemed unlikely indeed, with a convoy of ducks making their way determinedly over to her, and the soft strangling coo of a pigeon and the demented shriek of the cockerel still the only sounds in the early-morning hush.

Summer settled herself on the bottom of one of the upturned boats and let her mind dwell on her good fortune. To find a job when she was a stranger and totally inexperienced was good enough, but to enjoy it, as she had enjoyed waiting at table the previous evening, was the icing on the cake. She wondered why Nell had left, though. A quarrel with the boss was nasty and he seemed the type with whom it would be all too easy to disagree, but to leave just because of it? Castlebridge was a charming place, the job agreeable, the other girls very pleasant, but perhaps Nell had heard of a better job and wanted to go. It was no concern of hers, anyway. She had not taken Nell's job, Nell had thrown the job up. All she had to do was to enjoy it and work hard at it so that she could feel her time here had been used to good effect.

Summer was meeting Felix at noon, when she came off duty. They would, she supposed, try to find her notecase first. She glanced up and across the water, towards the track by which she had entered the village, and found that she had no desire to retrace her steps. Surprised by such stupidity, for Caliban was probably miles away by now, she had a short, sharp word with herself. You're dumb and a moron, she scolded, kicking out at the water to make her point and sending an arc of drops glistening into the air. No one, not even Caliban, really lives in caves! He'll have gone home last night, or if not home, to his own tent or caravan or whatever, and probably he wouldn't recognize you anyway if you came face to face, nor you him.

But the last, she knew, was not true. She would know that low hairline, those simian features, anywhere! He might have been trying to tell her she had dropped her notecase once they left his private plateau, if he thought of it as that, but at first he had been too furious over her prying, or whatever he called it, to worry about anything else.

I ought to go back right now, whilst it's quiet, and take a look, Summer said severely to herself, and kicked up another arc of spray to emphasize the point. On the other hand, Felix had said he would go with her, why not enjoy his company again? It was, she supposed, the effects of adversity, but she had not once felt shy, ill at ease, stupid or homely whilst with Felix. She had just felt normal, as she did when she and her best friend, Sally-Ann, were having a chat over a milkshake down at the drug-store, or even in school, perched on a hard chair, their heads close together, ostensibly studying but sometimes catching up on interesting gossip.

Having decided that she would wait until Felix was with her before trying to find the notecase, it seemed idle to sit by the water any longer; after all, she had set out intending to explore the village so she would do just that. Summer got up off the boat, stretched, and walked back the way she had come. Even in the short time she had been gone the village had woken up. A black cat, tail erect, eyes gleaming yellow, walked precisely across the road towards her. A fat old spaniel poddled about outside the gift shop, and inside the shop someone whistled as they moved quietly around. A man, elderly but upright, walked briskly along the sidewalk. He nodded to Summer, then went into the shop. Summer, following for something to do, discovered that the shop sold newspapers and candy as well as gifts. The elderly man was buying a newspaper from the girl Summer recognized as being Beryl Bloxham, the proprietor's daughter. She was perhaps a couple of years older than Summer herself with a quantity of peroxided hair and a heavy, sulky mouth, and she bore, so far as Summer could see, absolutely no resemblance to her father.

The elderly man was chatting and Summer moved up behind him, mindful of the slender means at her disposal. She did not intend to squander her

35

money on a newspaper, but there was a good display of candy and she was hungry. If they weren't expensive, she would splash out on some. Felix had lent her a fiver until she was paid and she still had almost three pounds of her own money left, so she could afford some mints and a candy bar – a Marathon would be nice.

She was still choosing, in her mind, when a familiar name caught her ear and brought her attention to the customer in front of her. He was still speaking.

'. . . not much loss in one way, I daresay, that Nell,' he was saying rather crossly. 'Had no time for an old codger like me, but my money was good enough! Couldn't catch her eye when I wanted more hot water for my tea or another slice of toast, but when I wanted to pay the bill she was always there, right on time, hand held out!'

'She was a good waitress,' Beryl said grudgingly. 'Fast, and that. But of course always chasing after the lads, just as if . . .'

The elderly customer cut across her without an apology; he was obviously a man with a grievance so far as Nell was concerned.

'Fast she certainly was! Ho dear me, yes, fast is the very word! When I sat with young Felix or Harry, then she was all over me, ho yes, I did notice that! And there was that scruffy little chap who delivers beer and so on – I saw them . . .'

'Them?' It was not Beryl who had spoken, but the proprietor. Summer had scarcely noticed him save as a silent figure, cigarette drooping from the corner of his mouth, moving about in the back room sorting papers, but apparently he had been listening to the conversation for now he came right into the shop, head cocked, eyes hard. 'Them?' he repeated. 'What did you mean by that, colonel?'

'Why, that young Nell and her fellers,' the colonel

said, looking rather surprised at the proprietor's sudden interest. 'Morning, Bloxham, didn't see you beavering away in the back there. Just saying, saw Nell with that feller . . . scruffy chap . . . who delivers beer. I was walking Gypsy, giving the old girl some exercise up in the hills . . . not too much, mind, because I don't walk like I used to, not since my accident,' he patted his knee meaningly and pulled a face. 'Gives me a bad time on hills.'

'You saw Nell and the delivery man,' prompted Mr Bloxham. 'You were saying, colonel?'

But the colonel, it appeared, was no longer interested in Nell or her young men. He clicked his tongue impatiently and pointed to the paper which Beryl had been about to hand him.

'What's that, m'dear gal? I want my *Telegraph*, not the damned *Times*! I have the *Times* at the weekend, not on a weekday!'

Beryl did not reply but turned to change the newspaper for one on the pile behind her. Her father, however, persisted.

'You were saying, colonel, that you'd seen Nell and the delivery man . . .'

'Yes, I've said it twice,' the colonel said irascibly. 'For God's sake, man, I've *told* you. Do listen when a chap speaks!' He turned to Beryl. 'Put the paper on my order, and I'll have one of those bars of chocolate with the air in 'em. Gypsy's fond of them and when she knows I've a bit of chocolate in my pocket I don't have to worry that she'll make off.' He smiled and wagged his head, selecting a fair-sized bar of chocolate from the display. 'She can be a naughty girl, can Gypsy, but she's just like a child, really. Show her sweeties and everything else goes out of her head.'

Summer could see that the proprietor wanted to continue to try to get the old man to explain something more about Nell and the delivery man, but Beryl, obviously realizing the same thing, put a detaining hand on her father's arm and shook her head.

'I'll put the chocolate on your account too, colonel,' she said soothingly. 'Gypsy ran in ahead of you earlier, full of spirits. Did you take her far into the hills yesterday? A long walk?'

Summer was amused to see this ploy being tried, but it was tried in vain. The colonel, it seemed, was a trifle deaf. He was carrying a walking stick which he raised in jocular salute as he turned to leave the shop, first tucking the chocolate well down into the pocket of his tweed jacket.

'Yes, a fine morning for a walk. Good day to you both.'

Summer moved forward to take his place at the counter and was surprised to find Beryl fixing her with a baleful glance.

'Oh, it's you, I didn't see you! Why aren't you next door?'

'It's too early for breakfast,' Summer said diffidently. 'I came out for a bit of air, that's all. I'm kinda hungry, so I thought I'd have one of those.' She pointed to the pile of Marathon bars, neatly stacked.

Beryl picked one of the bars up and held it out, giving it an impatient shake when Summer did not immediately take it from her.

'Come on then, if you want it! But they'll be serving staff breakfast quite soon.'

Summer put the money down on the counter and took her candy bar, then turned away to leave the shop. Behind her, an altercation broke out between father and daughter. Only half listening, she guessed that Mr Bloxham was blaming Beryl for something and that Beryl was defending herself by attacking her father.

'. . . never do know how to get things out of people without putting their backs up,' Beryl was saying. 'Anyway, I don't see that it matters if the old boy saw them carrying on together. She always was . . .'

Poor Nell, Summer reflected, taking a big bite of Marathon and turning up the little alley around the back of the cafe. She probably left because Beryl had it in for her. She had gathered, from the conversation of the other waitresses the previous evening, that Nell had been head waitress and a force to be reckoned with, sometimes an unpopular and disliked force, indeed. No one seemed to know or care why she had left, but almost everyone had indicated, at some time during the evening, that her leaving was a good thing and that Summer herself was a welcome change from Nell.

She found the five-barred gate open, though she had shut it, and the back door, too, gaped wide. Summer went into the room, to find a woman in a checked wrapover mopping the floor. She looked up and smiled as she saw Summer conscientiously trying to avoid the wet patches, stopping work for a moment to sigh and shake her head.

'It'll be mired by noon, ducks, so don't worry where you're treading. You the new waitress, then?'

'That's right. I'm Summer Campion. Good morning, Mrs . . . er . . .'

'Violet Samson. The girls call me Vi.'

'Good morning, Vi. What can I do to help you? Shall I start in the cafe? The door was locked when I came down first thing, but I see it's open now.'

The woman smiled and resumed her work, the mop moving in large, bubbly circles over the tiles.

'That's all right, you don't start till later. First you get your breakfast wi' t'other lasses.'

Summer saw that the kitchen table was covered

with various foods and that in the cafe four tables had been pulled together and were set out with crockery and cutlery for several persons. A heavily built woman in a white apron with her hair tied up in a white linen square was frying a gigantic pile of bacon; tomatoes spat from a smaller pan and, on another ring, beans bubbled gently. The kettle was whistling plaintively so Summer went across and turned the gas down, then addressed the cook, who she had met the previous evening.

'Anything I can do for you, Mrs Shaw?'

It was at once clear from Mrs Shaw's expression that she was not a morning person. She scowled blackly, first at the bacon in her frying pan and then at Summer.

'No. Made your bed? Done your room out?'

'Oh! Well, no, I'm afraid . . .'

'It's all to be done before you come down.' Mrs Shaw shook the pan and forked a crisped piece of bacon out on to a white pot plate. 'If you aren't down here in fifteen minutes prompt I can't answer for you being fed this morning.'

'Oh!' Summer said again. 'Well . . . should I go up again, then?'

The woman grunted and Summer decided to accept it as the only sort of civil answer she was likely to get and left the kitchen, running quickly up the stairs. Sounds of stirring from the other rooms showed that her fellow waitresses were not early risers, and the small, old-fashioned bathroom was empty. She slipped in, washed and cleaned her teeth, went to her own room for jeans instead of cut-offs and then, having dragged the covers over her bed in a way which would have brought an outraged cry from her mother, she decided to empty her backpack into the chest of drawers.

The first drawer was empty save for lining paper. Summer put her thick sweater in it. The second one was also empty so she stowed away her denims, two pairs of cut-offs and her socks. In the last drawer she would keep underwear and shirts.

She was just about to put three shirts in when she noticed it was not quite as empty as she had thought. Something was rucking up the lining paper at the back of the drawer.

Summer lifted the paper and fished out the object which proved to be one of those little packets of sugar which some cafes give their customers. Usually such packets have the name of the company on them or even the name of the cafe but this one had a small brightly coloured picture on it. Closer inspection showed it was of Lake Windermere, a colour photo showing the lake in spring with the trees around it bright with new leaf. Summer had not known they made scenic sugar packets and wondered if there was one of Castlebridge and this particular lake. If so, it would be a nice memento. But since Windermere was of no particular interest to her she screwed the little packet up – it was empty – and looked for a waste-paper basket in which to chuck it.

There was none, so Summer threw it into her now rapidly emptying backpack and turned to the drawer again, smiling to herself. She had been building up a picture of Nell as bad-tempered and bossy, now she could add a more human touch; despite the size of last night's meal, Nell must have been a secret snacker. Or perhaps she had liked sweet things and had added extra sugar to her hot drink at night. Summer had been given a mug of drinking chocolate the previous evening to take up to bed with her. It had been quite sweet enough for her taste but perhaps not for Nell's.

Spreading the lining paper flat again, Summer put her shirts into the drawer and shut it, then turned and kicked her backpack under the bed. Just as it slid from sight someone knocked on her door. She called 'Come in!', and the door opened in order that Sandy might poke her head around the edge.

'Ready, Summer? We're going down for breakfast. We usually go together because old Ma Shaw doesn't half get ratty in the mornings if you're a split second late. And it makes her nasty for the rest of the day if she's really in a mood.'

'She's already had a go at me,' Summer confessed, crossing the room and descending the stairs behind Sandy and Fay, another waitress who had worked with Summer the previous evening. 'Is she always like that?'

'She is in the mornings,' Fay confirmed, smiling up over her shoulder as they thundered down the second flight of stairs. She was a small, brown girl with hazel eyes, tanned skin and a square and solid physique. 'By lunchtime she's human, more or less – if no one's annoyed her by being late for breakfast, that is – but by the evening she's beginning to get crabby again because her feet give her gyp after a day standing at the cooker.'

'Right, I'll remember that.' The small group turned left at the foot of the stairs and went through the door into the kitchen, where Mrs Shaw was now squared up for action, with plates spread out and bacon, tomato and beans already on most of them, whilst she served eggs straight from the spitting pan on to rounds of bread, to complete the meal. 'What do we do? Just take a plate each?'

'That's it. Then go through into the cafe. Our tables will be set and ready for us. Mrs Shaw sits at the head and pours the tea.'

'No coffee?' Summer tried not to sound plaintive, but the other girls laughed.

'What, at the price that is? No fear! Tea's all right, any road; it's what most of us'ud get at home.'

Summer took her place at the table, between Sandy and Fay, and watched as the others joined them. There was Beryl Bloxham and her father, who came and sat with the staff quite happily, or so it seemed, and there was Vi, who waddled in beaming at the sight of breakfast, and then Mrs Shaw of course. Just as they all seemed settled, another girl wandered in, yawning behind her hand.

'Morning,' she said, sliding into her seat. 'Late, am I? Still, you've not started.'

She was older than the other waitresses, and prettier, too, with shoulder-length, shining chestnut hair in a swinging pageboy style. Everyone chorused good morning and Summer was just thinking, rather aggrievedly, that this girl did not seem to mind at all about being late, when Mr Bloxham spoke to her.

'Angela, you know our new girl? Summer, this is Angela. She and Nell shared head-waitressing, so you'll mind her, won't you?'

Guessing that an affirmative was required, Summer nodded and murmured obediently, though she could not see how Angela would affect her. She liked the look of the older girl though, particularly when Angela winked at her across the table and said softly, 'I was having my day off yesterday, so you wouldn't have seen me, in case you're wondering where I sprang from. How did you get on with Nell?'

'I only came last evening, and she left before then,' Summer said, and was surprised when Angela looked puzzled.

'Left?' She turned to Mr Bloxham. 'Where's Nell gone, then?'

'Flounced off,' Mr Bloxham said briefly, chewing bacon and speaking rather thickly through a mouthful. 'We 'ad words.'

'You did?' Angela sighed and took the cup of tea nearest her. 'This mine? So she's gone, then?'

'That's right.'

'Not for good, though?'

'Well, she didn't say she'd be coming back.' Mr Bloxham finished his mouthful, took a slurp of his tea, swallowed it and then spoke again. 'Don't suppose we'll ever see Nell again; too high and mighty for the likes of us.'

After that the conversation became general once again and very soon the plates were cleared and the girls went about their business.

It was soon evident to Summer that working in the cafe was no sinecure: the breakfast rush was a reality, not wishful thinking. Hikers who had spent the night in tents came in for a good meal, while others who had caught an early train up from a big city came in to get their stomachs lined before starting the day ahead. The girls scurried about until, at eleven o'clock or so, the rush for what the British called 'a full house' seemed to be slackening, and then the coffees started.

These customers were older and usually came in cars which they parked down on the big car park by the lake. Then they strolled up into the village, frequented the gift shop, bought a few things perhaps, and then came into the cafe for coffee, cakes, biscuits or scones.

When noon came and Angela called her over, Summer was glad just to stop running for a moment. She took off her frilly pinafore and blew out her cheeks in a whistle of amazement.

'Angela, isn't it *busy*? We simply didn't stop, all

44

morning, and now I suppose they'll start coming in for main meals.'

Angela nodded and grinned sympathetically.

'That's right, but you needn't bother about it. Go through and have your meal and then you're off until eight this evening. Liz will take over your tables, and Cath will take over from Sandy. At eight, come and see me. All right?'

'Sure, fine,' Summer said thankfully. 'We get a meal now, do we?'

'That's right. Either in the kitchen, if Mrs Shaw isn't too rushed, or at the end table in the cafe if she is.'

Summer went into the kitchen, was given a meal, and took it back into the cafe. She had barely settled herself at the table with Sandy and with a fat, cross-eyed kitchen helper whose name she did not catch, when out of the corner of her eye she saw Felix enter the room. He smiled across and raised a hand, then strolled to the counter and after a few moments came over to their table and pulled up a chair.

'Mind if I join you, girls? I'm not having much, just a snack.'

Everyone, it seemed, liked Felix. The kitchen helper's face, round and puddingy though it was, lit up when he joined them and Sandy offered to share her chips. Summer, who would willingly have handed her french fries over and the delicious chicken pie as well, for she felt Felix very much her benefactor, was forced to watch enviously as he dipped lean fingers into Sandy's chips, salted them and ate them. But he included her in the light, casual conversation and as soon as she put her knife and fork down on the plate he, too, stood up.

'Well, nice to see you, girls. Summer and I are off to explore,' he said, putting a proprietorial hand under Summer's elbow and leading her out of the cafe. 'I'll bring her back to you safe and sound for her evening shift.' Summer, catching a glimpse of the faces she had left, saw, astonishingly, that envy was writ plain on each countenance. Envy? Of *her*? Surely they could not think that Felix wanted her company for any reason other than the most mundane? But it was nice, even so, to be envied. Summer felt a new layer of self-confidence covering up her normal doubts.

Outside, in the sunshine, Felix let go of her arm and surveyed her thoughtfully.

'Jeans? Nice for work but not so nice for hiking. Look, we're going to see if we can find your notecase, right? But that won't take all afternoon. Go and change into something cooler, and bring a swimsuit. We'll go for a swim when we get back.'

'Right,' Summer said. She hurried into the building and was back in no more than five or six minutes, her swimsuit wrapped in a towel reposing inside her delightfully light backpack.

'You came down that path, I suppose?' Felix pointed and, when Summer agreed, the two of them set out.

'In half an hour or so, you may be your old wealthy self,' Felix said as the track began to climb the side of the hill. 'You'll be able to give up your job and move on, if you want to.'

Summer laughed. She did not tell him that she had no intention of moving on. Having found a congenial companion and a pleasant job, she would remain in Castlebridge until her godmother's return to her home, even if she was lucky enough to find her notecase with the money in it intact.

An hour later, standing on the very plateau on which, the previous day, she had first seen Caliban,

Summer ruefully concluded that the question of leaving Castlebridge was unlikely to arise. Though she and Felix had searched the track most carefully, they had not seen any sign of her notecase and the plateau itself contained nothing other than boulders, grass and dust. She had tried, naturally, to retrace her path down the hillside, but it was impossible. Every tree, every boulder, every blade of grass, was so similar to its brother that identification was out of the question. There were a score of ways in which she might have left the plateau, a score of different routes she might have taken. She and Felix split up and combed the area to the best of their ability but either the notecase had been spotted and picked up by someone else or it lay, neglected and unseen, beneath some clump of foliage past which they had not even walked.

'I'm about ready to call it a day,' Felix remarked presently. He touched Summer's shoulder, then snatched his hand back as she winced, the burn still not completely cured. 'Sorry, I forgot. Look, we've given it a good hour, longer in fact, and we've not even managed to find the way you took, running downhill. Guess we'll have to consider your money gone.'

'I don't mind,' Summer said, smiling at him, seeing him despondent for the first time in their short acquaintance. 'Gee, Felix, I lost the thing yesterday. I accepted I'd lost it then, this was just . . . well, just a vain hope.'

'Yeah. It's a shame, but . . .' He brightened. 'Tell you what, let's do a reconstruction of the crime, shall we?'

'A reconstruction? I don't get it.'

'Well, last time you ran like crazy because you were frightened, right?'

'Sure.'

'This time you won't be frightened, but I want you

47

to *act* scared, see? Come round the boulder the way you described it, see me, back off, then turn and run fast as you can . . . We'll see if it pays off and you take your original track. Were you heading for the path, that first time?'

'Yes, kind of. Only like you said, I ran blind . . . I just wanted to get away.'

'Then do the same this time.' Felix crossed the plateau and squatted by the flat-topped boulder in the manner Summer had described when telling him about the encounter with Caliban. 'Now I'm laying my cards out . . .' He fished in his pocket, produced his wallet and placed, on the flat surface before him, various cards, notes and other objects. 'Go away, Summer, then come back, peer round at me, and try to imagine I'm Caliban.'

Summer did as she was told, feeling remarkably silly. As if she could possibly lose her head the way she had before, when she knew this time they were just play-acting. But she obeyed Felix, coming round the boulder and, to tell the truth, getting quite a turn when she saw only the top of his dark head and his moving hands, for he looked uncannily like Caliban just for a moment.

She moved, and Felix looked up. He stared at her and his eyes grew hard and cold. He jumped to his feet, shouting . . . and suddenly it was not a game any longer, it was real, it was not Felix who stood there but Caliban and she must run and run and get right away from him or . . .

She ran down the hillside like a deer, leaping obstacles, dodging others, her breath panting in her throat, her heart thundering in her ears. Far below her was the track – she must get to the track – and close behind her came her pursuer, she could see the cloud of dust raised by his progress out of the corner of her eye.

She forgot the notecase, their purpose in staging this reconstruction; she thought only of escape. When she saw the boulders and the rowan trees she flung herself sideways in amongst them, dodged through them and cast herself instinctively at the shielding and enveloping gorse bushes which clustered at the foot of the cliff face.

And Felix – as Caliban had – ran straight past, hesitated . . . she could hear voices from the track, as she had heard them yesterday . . . and then turned back, making for the plateau once more.

Only this time it was different . . . wasn't it? This was only her friend Felix. Now he was coming back, dodging the boulders as she had done, calling her name . . . and Summer crouched lower for an instant, her heart beating even faster at his approach, before she forced herself to stand up.

Slowly, reluctantly almost, she pushed her way through the surrounding gorse.

'Felix, here I am!' she called.

4

'It was real weird, to see you panic like that,' Felix said slowly, as the two of them made their way back to the track. 'Guess you let yourself believe I was Caliban?'

'You looked at me so hard and cold, just like he did,' Summer confessed. 'And once I started running it was as if he was behind me, not you at all.'

'Yeah, I tried to pretend you were my Great-Aunt Florence, the meanest, most evil-minded lady I know,' Felix said, giving her a rueful grin. 'But . . . you were real scared, not pretend scared.'

'I know. I told you . . .'

'I know what you told me. I didn't believe you were that afraid, though,' Felix said slowly. His hand came down gently and rested on her shoulder; it was still a bit sore but Summer did not wince. It was bad enough to run, all but shrieking, when she had known very well it was only Felix behind her and that the chase was not serious. It would not do to be chicken over a sore shoulder into the bargain! 'Summer, what did you think he'd do to you if he caught you up?'

'Do you want the shameful truth, or can I lie a bit?'

Felix laughed and squeezed her shoulder. Summer drew in her breath sharply but made no other sign. Why had she been such a fool as to let herself get burnt, that was the question!

'The truth, girl!'

'I thought he'd either beat me up or kill me. It isn't as stupid as it sounds, either. We were a long way from other people and assaults go on everywhere these days, even in England.'

'You're right, and if anyone's stupid, it's me. So he was a tough cookie, hey? The sort that won't think twice before using his fists?'

'Yes, that's right. He would have enjoyed it.'

They had not found the notecase in their breathless, tumbling race down the hillside. Summer had not looked, but Felix had kept his wits about him and afterwards they had carefully followed the track she had taken right up to the plateau and down again with no luck. Now, with Felix's hand still resting lightly on Summer's shoulder, they stepped down on the track again. Summer waited for Felix to move away from her as a group of youngsters approached, but instead he steered her to one side and they continued to descend, Summer trying hard to look as though she frequently walked along with a guy's hand on her shoulder.

'Now you said Caliban was scruffy. I thought of a hiker, someone like that. Was I right?'

'No! He was wearing a white singlet, only it was pretty dirty, more grey than white, and it had a hole in one side. He had baggy old brown work-pants on held up by a leather belt. The pants were all stained, too. And he was wearing sneakers, old ones. One of them had string instead of a lace.'

'That description sounds familiar.' Felix frowned down at his feet as they strolled along. 'Now where have I seen a guy with one dirty sneaker tied together with string? I know, about a week ago I saw Nell walking up this very track with a meathead she'd picked up somewhere. I'd almost swear he'd string in one sneaker.'

'Oh, but could it really be the same one?' Summer asked. 'It seems unlikely. Did he look as though he was the type to play with cards?'

'Yeah, I forgot the cards.' Felix looked down at her, his eyes bright and intent. 'What sort of game was he playing, Summer? Snap? Patience?'

'He wasn't playing cards, I don't think, he was playing *with* them,' Summer tried to explain. 'He was engrossed all right, but he was picking them up and putting them down . . . fiddling with them more than actually playing a game.'

'Hmm. What'll you do if he walks into the cafe and wants a meal?'

'Make an excuse and get out until he's gone,' Summer said unhesitatingly. 'I don't want to meet him again.'

'You think he'll still be angry? Like he was on the plateau?'

'I guess not,' Summer said in a small voice. 'I guess I really am being stupid now, but I really don't want to meet him again.'

'If your instinct says he's dangerous then you're probably right and you should steer clear of him,' Felix agreed. 'The question is, honey, why was he fit to smash you in? What did you *do*, for Christ's sake?'

'Nothing! All I did was see him there, messing about with those cards, or whatever,' Summer said positively. 'I didn't do anything.'

'Perhaps it was just seeing him that was wrong,' Felix said after a frowning pause. 'Perhaps he shouldn't have been there. Perhaps the cards weren't his – if they were cards.'

'I don't know, but does it matter? I'm never likely

to see him again and he probably won't come into the cafe. I've lost my money but by the end of the week I'll have earned enough to make up and I'm having a good time as well. Can't we leave it at that?'

'Sure we can. It's just so damn weird! I didn't think it mattered, Summer, until I realized that guy really had you running scared. And then I got to wondering . . .' He gave her shoulder a little shake then dropped his hand to his side. 'Aw, I'm being paranoid, I guess. It was when I started thinking there were two odd things. First you being chased for no good reason and then Nell up and leaving. She doesn't seem to have told anyone she was going. Probably it doesn't matter, though.'

'I shouldn't think it matters at all,' Summer said, as they neared the village. 'The girls seem to think she had a row with Ozzie.' Ozzie was the girls' name for Mr Bloxham. 'He's real mean when he wants, he could make a girl cut and run, I'm sure.'

'Yeah, and Nell could be pretty mean too, if she felt inclined. Still, it's none of my business, I guess.' He stopped, a hand on her arm, and gestured ahead of them, to a group of pines by the roadside. 'Down there, through those trees, there's a bit of shore hardly anyone visits. We'll bathe there, shall we, and then lie in the sun for a bit. You've got your things, haven't you?'

'Yes, and a towel.' Together, they made their way through the trees and emerged presently on to a small beach. There were a few large rocks and Summer changed behind one; Felix did not have to change, he was wearing swimming trunks beneath his jeans. Then they splashed quickly into the water, which was surprisingly chilly at first gasp, and swam and enjoyed themselves, feeling cool and fresh, in Summer's case at least, for the first time since their expedition had started.

Afterwards, they lay on the beach and talked.

Summer told Felix about her life in New York; about her mother, their apartment, her school and her father. Felix, in return, told her about his own life back home and a bit about the course he was on and the guys he was friendliest with.

'I was real lucky getting a place here,' he said lazily, one arm up across his face to shield his eyes from the sun. 'I'm starting my last year in September and at the end of it I'll have my degree and a year's practical experience and I'll be ready to go back home and show 'em all.'

'Why did you come over here?' Summer said idly. 'I came for the history course first off, and then because my father was born and brought up in Britain and only left when he was seventeen. He met my mom in the Lake District years and years ago, and they were good friends. Then when he went to the States he looked her up again and later on they were married. So I suppose you could say if it wasn't for the Lake District, I wouldn't be here at all.'

'I came here on an exchange scholarship,' Felix explained. 'Some guy from Hatfield is over in the U.S. right now, doing the same 's me but in reverse. My Pa's got an engineering works, but I didn't want to go straight in with him, I wanted to do something a bit different, so I'll get my degree and then decide exactly how to use it.'

The conversation then turned to other things, and time really went by at speed so that when Summer glanced at her watch and saw it was almost seven o'clock she sat up with a jerk, dismayed at the thought of being late.

'Gee, Felix, look at the time!' She scrambled to her feet, flushed and sandy. 'I must get back, I've got to be cleaned up and downstairs again by eight for the evening shift.'

'Right.' Felix got up too and sprinted down to the water. 'Come on, a last dip to get the muck off us!'

They swam briefly, then jog-trotted back to the village, to part outside the cafe.

'See you tomorrow,' Felix called, as he headed for his lodgings. 'I'll come in for breakfast!'

'See you,' echoed Summer. She hurried round the back of the building and in through the kitchen door. Mrs Shaw was at the height of the evening rush and scarcely grunted as Summer hurried past, but Liz spotted her and waved.

'Hi, luv! Have a nice time?'

'It was great,' Summer said. 'We forgot the time, but I'll be down in a tick to give you a hand.'

'It's all right, no rush.' That was Angela, coming through from the cafe, her tray heavy with dirty crockery. 'You aren't on for another twenty minutes or so. Make the most of your time off today, ducks, because tomorrow we'll all be rushed off our feet and you'll be lucky to get half an hour off for a spit and a drag.'

'Why? What's special about tomorrow?' Summer asked, pausing in the doorway.

'Coach in from the continent,' Angela explained briefly. 'They arrive here lunchtime, we feed 'em and then they're taken off to their campsite. It means forty-six more people at our busiest time of day as well as all our usual customers.'

'Oh? But that only lasts an hour or so, surely?'

Angela, unloading her tray into the dishwater, laughed hollowly. 'So you might well think! What it means is we're busy laying up extra tables all morning – whilst doing our ordinary work, of course – and then from the moment they leave we have all these aggrieved customers pouring in for late lunches and early teas . . . Well, you'll see for yourself in the morning.'

Summer laughed, nodded, and hurried off up the stairs, but when she reached her landing she was in for a surprise. She actually had her hand on her doorknob when she felt it turning beneath her fingers. Before she could do more than gasp, it opened and she found herself face to face with Beryl Bloxham!

'Oh, am I in the wrong room? I'm so sorry . . .' she began, but was interrupted by Beryl, whose face had gone an unhealthy shade of puce.

'Nell rang . . . she left something behind . . . I was just looking for her gold shell earrings.' She stared pointedly at Summer's own ears. 'I can't find them, so I wondered if you might have used them, seeing Nell had left.'

'No, indeed,' Summer said quickly. 'I couldn't, my ears aren't pierced. Where did you look?' She could not help hoping that Beryl had not been poking around in her drawers and taking note of all her small possessions. It would be too bad if Beryl concluded that all American girls travelled thousands of miles with only a few bits of underwear and some T-shirts and jeans, but Summer did not feel able to explain about her big suitcase in London, or the dozen or so thick jumpers and heavy skirts which her mother had insisted that she pack.

'Where? Why, she told me where she'd left them, of course, and I looked there.' Beryl's colour had faded but her expression was sharp and spiteful. 'What's it to you, Yank?'

'I wondered if you'd tried the bathroom, that's all,' Summer said, trying not to sound as angry as she felt. 'If you'd asked me, I'd have told you the bedroom had nothing of Nell's in it, except . . .'

She had been going to say, except for an empty sugar packet in one of the drawers but it sounded so petty and small that she decided to say nothing.

Beryl, however, raised her over-plucked brows, and her mean little eyes seemed to get even closer together than nature had placed them.

'What? Except for what?'

'Oh, nothing. I was only kidding, she didn't leave anything, really.'

'Come on, Yank, what did she leave? Whatever it was it should be sent on to her.'

Summer could not help smiling at the thought of sending on an empty sugar packet but she just shook her head.

'She didn't leave anything! Sorry, Beryl. If you don't mind, I'm due on in a few minutes, I must get changed.'

She pushed past the older girl and, when Beryl still continued to stand on the landing, staring in at her, she closed the door, gently but firmly, in the other's face.

When Summer joined the other girls for their ten o'clock meal, she was at first unaware of anything save for a sharp and healthy appetite and a great desire to get the weight off her feet. Because there were still customers in the cafe they ate in relays in the kitchen, and once she was settled the first thing Sandy said to her, leaning close and breathing heavily, was rather upsetting.

'I say, Summer, what on earth have you done to Beryl? She's got it in for you good and proper!'

'For me? Well, I don't see why! It wasn't me who was so fresh as to go into someone else's room . . . Did you know I found her there, searching for some earrings Nell had lost, she said?'

'You never! Cor, the cheek of some people! Mind you, she's a bit like that. You keep an eye on her tomorrow and you'll see all sorts.'

'What do you mean? I never see her during the day, unless I go into the gift shop for something.'

But at this point one of the other waitresses turned to Summer with a remark and Sandy shook her head, put a finger to her lips, and turned the conversation. When they had eaten, however, she invited Summer to accompany her for a breath of fresh air.

'We'll just walk down to the lake and back,' she said to Angela, who seemed quite capable of doing anyone's job and who was standing in for Mrs Shaw right now and cooking all the snacks and hot drinks being ordered. 'We won't be more than ten minutes.'

'If it was Cath I'd know she wanted a fag, but I suppose you two really do want fresh air,' Angela said, smiling at them as she cracked eggs into the big black frying-pan. 'Well, don't be long, you know what the rush is like when the pubs turn out.'

Outside, in the mild, starlit dark, Sandy drew Summer down to sit on the bridge and to watch the gentle lappings and glintings of the water.

'I couldn't say too much in there,' she muttered, keeping her voice low. 'But when I first came here I thought our Beryl was a right little tea-leaf . . . that's thief to you . . .' she added, as Summer's expression remained blank. 'She isn't, though, she's just incredibly nosy and not at all averse to poking around in other people's possessions. You know when they take rucksacks into shops they're made to hand them over the counter so they don't break things when they turn round sharply?'

'Sure. And we take them in the cafe too, so they don't clutter up the aisles between the tables and break someone's leg.'

'That's it. Well, once I went through into the room at the back of the shop, where they pile up all the rucksacks, and there was Beryl, with her hands right down inside someone else's bag!'

'Well then, she *is* a thief!'

But Sandy was shaking her head, her fair, frizzy hair bobbing. 'No. She's just curious. There's never been a complaint that I've heard of. She probably goes through all our rooms when we're on duty, but you had the bad luck to catch her. That's why she's so angry with you, trying to get Ozzie to say you'll have to leave.'

Alarm shot through Summer. She did not want to leave – where would she go?

'To leave? Oh, Sandy, will they get rid of me, like Nell?'

'No, I'm sure you're okay. Ozzie told Beryl to shut her yap and leave the staff side of things to him. She pouted, but she stopped going on.'

'Gee, thank goodness. When was all this, anyway?'

'Just before you came down for your shift.'

Summer nodded. 'Yeah, that'll be because I found her in my room all right; she must have come straight down and started in on Ozzie then. Well, I'll be extra-polite to her in future and see if I can make up for catching her out!'

When the girls returned from their short walk, both Mr Bloxham and Beryl were in the kitchen, getting themselves a meal which they would carry through into the cafe. Mr Bloxham greeted them normally and even Beryl, with her father's eye upon her, managed to make a pretence of being civil. Summer, for her part, behaved like a thorough-going creep. She carried their tray of tea through for them, went back for sugar and then again for extra hot water, and told Mr Bloxham that she thought Castlebridge must be the prettiest village she had ever

59

seen and the gift shop easily the best-stocked little store she'd visited.

'You can be a smarmy little sod when you like,' Sandy said approvingly, as the two of them, giggling, helped Angela to put away the last of the dishes once the cafe was closed. 'Mind, I thought you were laying it on a bit thick when you said you were going to save up your wages to buy those singing shepherdesses for all your aunts and cousins, but he lapped it up. Those shepherdesses were his own idea. He went all the way to Stoke-on-Trent where they're made and bought a job lot cheap, and of course he's not sold any! Rich tourists looking for tat don't come our way much.'

'They sure are awful,' Summer agreed, clattering plates. 'I was nearly struck dumb when I first saw one working.'

'Don't say that in front of all the girls,' Angela warned them, turning away from unloading the dishwasher yet again, to clatter a still-dirty pan into the sink. 'Some of 'em think the shepherdesses are great. Cath really does want one for her mother . . . the one that sings "Danny Boy" she says, being Irish.'

'I didn't know they sang different tunes,' Summer said. She had seen a china shepherdess, skirts outspread, lamb to heel, slowly rotating on her pedestal, whilst from that same pedestal came the tinkling tune of a popular folksong. 'Come to that, they don't really sing, they play, so why does he call them singing shepherdesses?'

Angela shrugged. 'Sounds better, I suppose. Now is one of you going to tell me why Summer's so busy buttering up Ozzie? Is it anything to do with the way Beryl attacked her, earlier in the evening?'

'That's it,' Summer said. 'She wants me out and I want me in, so I'm being nice. As for *why* she wants me out, we think, Sandy and me, that it's because I walked into my bedroom and caught her casing the joint.'

'Did you now? That'll explain it, then. Did she tell you what she was doing in there?'

'Nope. Well, she said she was searching for Nell's gold shell earrings. Said Nell had rung up about them, but I think she was just snooping, myself.'

'As if Nell would have spoken to Beryl, if she had rung up,' Angela scoffed. She cleared the dishwasher and moved over to the cooker. 'Why, everyone knows Nell and Beryl were scarcely on speaking terms! Though of course Beryl would know she was safe to tell you just about anything, being a newcomer!'

'I guess you're right. Well, anyway, if that's it, I'm off to bed. Can I take my hot drink up with me?'

'Certainly. And you as well, Sandy, or are you going to come through into the back room and watch telly for a bit?'

'No, I won't bother, I'm too tired,' Sandy said. 'I'll go up with Summer.' The two of them made their way up the long flights of stairs, but Sandy paused outside Summer's door for an explanation. 'They let us watch telly in the back room, evenings,' she told the other girl. 'It's quite fun, sometimes, but not this late, of course, because it'll be the news, or an old film. If you're off for the evening shift though, and you're feeling too tired for walking or swimming, then it's better than going to bed whilst it's still light.'

'I suppose so,' Summer said a trifle doubtfully. 'Are they always there? Ozzie and Beryl, I mean?'

'No, not always. Hardly ever, in fact. They've got a flat above the shop, you know, which is reached from the shop by a back staircase. Part of it is below us – that's why we have to go up two flights of stairs

61

and not just one. They have the middle floor.'

'I see.' Summer opened her door and clicked the light switch. 'Well, goodnight, Sandy, see you in the morning. Will you knock on my door, please, as you go to the bathroom? I'm tired but I dare not risk being late down.'

' 'Course I will,' Sandy said easily. 'Goodnight, Summer. Sweet dreams!'

Summer was dreaming, and a very mad, wild sort of dream it was too. She was out on the hillside first of all, watching Caliban playing cards with Felix, both dressed in waitress uniform of dark skirts, white blouses and frilly pinnies. They seemed quite amicable and then all at once Felix accused Caliban of cheating, and Caliban shouted and another waitress, who Summer knew at once to be Nell, appeared round the nearest boulder. She was very large and held a stick in one hand. She had a policeman's helmet perched on top of her head.

'Order, order,' she said sternly, reminding Summer of somebody or something, she could not quite think what. 'Whose deal is it?'

'Mine, mine,' both men shouted, and Caliban reached out and scooped all Felix's cards over to his own side of the rock. To Felix's rage and consternation Caliban then proceeded to tear the cards along one end, tip them up and eat the contents . . . and Summer realized they were not cards at all but packets of sugar.

'Stop that!' Nell ordered sharply. 'I'm the one who likes sugar,' and she hit Caliban on the head with her stick. Caliban roared, Felix stood up, and then Summer was running, running, leaping and bounding down the hillside, and then she was falling, over the edge of a mighty precipice, and the wind whistled in her ears, falling and falling . . .

She woke, considerably shaken, in her own bed, with sunlight pouring in and someone knocking on the door.

'Wakey wakey, Summer,' Sandy's voice called. 'Bathroom's free.'

Summer got shakily out of bed and hurried into the bathroom; it smelt of Sandy's soap and talc and there was a line across the room with several pairs of tights dangling wetly over the bath. It was too late for a shower and, in any case, the shower was one of those long rubber hoses which are attached to the taps and could prove fiendishly difficult to regulate as Summer had already discovered, so she tore off her nightie, had a quick, all-over rub down, and then hurried back to her room to don a clean T-shirt and jeans once more.

Making her way down to breakfast with Sandy and Cath this time – Fay was on a later shift and had decided to skip the meal and have a good lie-in instead – Summer thought about her dream. What rubbish it had been, and how strange that she should have dreamed about Nell, someone she had never actually met. It was a shame that, having dreamed about Felix, she could not have managed something a bit more romantic, but that was dreams for you. There was an old joke she'd heard years ago, in high school, about a guy who dreams he's in some famous harem . . . the only snag being that he's a woman too. That was the equivalent, Summer thought wryly, of dreaming of Felix but putting him into a waitress's uniform! Not that the girls in the cafe wore any uniform apart from the frilly white pinafores, for they did not. It was how she thought of English waitresses, she supposed vaguely, joining the other girls at the now-familiar breakfast table in the cafe.

'Morning, Summer.' The words came from several

people and Summer, smiling and answering, thought how nice it was that this group had accepted her so easily, without question. Different from the history group, who had been rather patronizing really, because of her youth.

Beryl and Ozzie were already at the table and Summer shot a glance across at Beryl, but the older girl was eating cornflakes and seemed to have forgotten her obsession with Summer; at least she did not look up, far less scowl and mutter.

Presently, however, Ozzie addressed her.

'Summer, you're free until noon. Then you're on until eight and free after that. Understand?'

'Sure.' Summer scraped back her chair and stood up. 'I'll go off now, then, unless there's anything I should do first?'

Angela, eating toast and marmalade with enthusiasm, flapped a hand at her, swallowed, coughed, and then spoke.

'Gracious, why do I always have something to say when my mouth's impossibly full? Summer, we've got a coach party booked in for twelve o'clock, so if you could possibly arrive say ten minutes early, I'd be grateful. That way, we'll have ten minutes to sort out tables and learn the specials on the menu before the worst of the rush starts.'

'Sure, glad to,' Summer said, heading for the door. 'See you all later!'

Outside, it was sunny again. Summer headed straight for the bridge, but Felix was not perched on the parapet. However, she hung around for a couple of minutes, admiring a tasteful display of patent medicines in the chemist's window, then Felix came out of his lodgings, saw her and came over.

'Hi! Have you eaten yet?'

'Yup. You?'

'Sure, I eat with the family but I meant to pop into the cafe for a coffee. Still, as you're out here, I suppose you aren't serving on the first shift?'

'Too right. There's a coach party coming in at noon and I'm on then and for the next eight hours. Say, Felix, waitresses earn their money!'

'Yeah, so I've heard. And I'm on at half eight until half four, which means we shan't be seeing much of each other until late evening.' Gratifyingly, he pulled a face. 'Still, no use beefing. With luck you'll be free when I am tomorrow.'

'We could go for a walk, perhaps, when I'm free at eight,' Summer suggested, highly daring, but Felix shook his head.

'You'll be too tired for walking, honey, if you've been on your feet for eight hours. But in fact I've had an idea. Do you know if any of the girls know Nell's home address? It's in the Keswick area, I believe.'

'Her home address? I wouldn't know, but I guess I could ask.'

Felix, however, shook his head.

'No, don't do that. I know 'em all, I'll have a quiet word with someone and see if I can find out. My boss is going into Keswick later today, to get some auto parts. I thought maybe I'd go along for the ride and see if I can find out just why Nell left.'

'I suppose someone'll know her address,' Summer said. 'By the way, I found Beryl in my room yesterday, going through my things. She said she was searching for Nell's earrings, if you can believe that!'

'I don't know what I believe,' Felix admitted, scratching his dark head. 'I just think it's weird she's left the way she seems to have done. And weird that Beryl was going through your things, and weird that . . .'

'The girls say Beryl's nosy and goes through

everyone's belongings, even the customers', ' Summer protested. 'Once you start thinking one thing is wrong, then everything seems wrong. I'm sure that's all it is.'

'You're probably right. If you are, then a word with Nell will convince me that I'm making bricks without straw or whatever the expression is. And anyway, I haven't been to Keswick for a while, it'll do me good to see city lights again.'

'Oh, right. Only the girls are a good crowd, Felix. If there was any reason to worry over Nell they'd do it, believe me. And I've almost forgotten Caliban, so don't go chasing off to Keswick on my account!'

Felix laughed and shook his head at her.

'On your account! Truth is, I'm enjoying imagining a bit of a mystery, it'll stop my brain cells from stagnating or whatever brain cells do when the body is active but the mind isn't. Want any shopping done?'

'No money,' Summer reminded him, smiling. 'Tell you what, Felix, could you get me an airletter, d'you think? I'll drop Mom a line just in case Aunt Peggy gets in touch with her and they worry . . . not that it's likely since Mom's on vacation with friends and not at home.'

'I'll do that. If I'm back in time I'll come in for a coffee just before you knock off and tell you what happened and hand over your airletter. If I'm not there you'll know the boss got held up in Keswick and I'll see you tomorrow.'

'See you then,' Summer said, but Felix held out a hand.

'Walk home with me, pretty lady?'

Summer laughed but took his hand. It felt good, strong and reliable. They swung along the pavement until they reached the garage and then Felix released her, waved and went in through the big double doors. Summer watched until he was out of sight and then walked slowly back the way she had come. It was a while before she was on duty; she could go back and see if any of the girls were free, she supposed, but from what she had gathered they made their plans well in advance. She had much better amuse herself for a while.

Outside the chemist's shop she hesitated, wondering whether to go in for more sunburn lotion. She had just decided that she was unlikely to need more since her burns were healing well when the chemist himself appeared. He smiled at her.

'Good morning, my dear! Another lovely day. How's the sunburn?'

'Almost gone, thanks,' Summer said, gratified to be remembered. 'I wonder you recognize all your customers,' she added naively.

'I don't, but your hair is unforgettable,' the chemist said. 'Besides, you aren't just any customer, you're a fellow worker I understand. Aren't you waiting on in the cafe?'

'Sure. I don't remember you coming in, though,' Summer said thoughtfully. 'I can remember customers, because I know so few people.'

The chemist laughed. He had very clear blue eyes, Summer saw, and though his hair was grey he was not at all old-looking. He had a reliable, trustworthy sort of face, so different from the weasely Ozzie!

'Well now, that's nice as well, even though you noticed my absence rather than my presence. You're right, of course, I very rarely eat out because I have my own flat above the shop and do most of my own cooking. But when I'm serving behind the counter I look up now and then and see the waitresses moving

67

around through the side window of the cafe. It's difficult to recognize more than a female shape but you've
been in and out too much for a mere customer, so I
guessed you were waiting on. I saw you chatting to
Felix earlier, didn't I?'

Summer nodded bashfully. As she recalled, she
and Felix had been standing right outside the chemist's shop when she had been quizzing Felix about
visiting Nell. How awful if the chemist thought she
was jealous of Felix seeing another girl.

'He's a nice chap, Felix,' the chemist said. 'I heard
him mention Nell, didn't I? The girl who worked in
the cafe before you arrived.'

'He mentioned her,' Summer agreed. 'He's going
to Keswick so he thought he might look her up.'

'Yes, I thought so. An odd sort of girl, Nell. Sly
eyes,' the chemist said dreamily. 'Still, one mustn't
judge people by their appearance, must one? I didn't
realize Felix had an interest there.'

'No . . . was she pretty?' It was out before Summer knew it and the moment the words left her lips
she was appalled; how fresh could she get? The
chemist, however, took her remark at face value.

'Pretty? Yes, in a certain way. Untrustworthy,
though. Liable to tell tall stories to make herself interesting, or to put herself in the right. Not a popular
young lady, I'd say. Though it seems Felix liked her?'

'Oh, I don't think so, I'm sure not,' Summer said
quickly. 'It was only because she left so suddenly,
without a word. I think he was making a mystery
over nothing, myself . . . Only it is odd, wouldn't
you say, that she never said a word to the other girls?'

'Yes, that is odd.' The chemist looked at Summer
as though he was about to say something, then
looked away; he had thought better of it. Then he
looked back and spoke quickly and so quietly that

Summer had to lean closer to listen. 'Does Felix think anything else at the cafe is a bit weird? That girl, the Bloxham girl, for instance?'

'Oh, she's just curious,' Summer said at once, unwilling to admit that not only Felix found some things about the Bloxham establishment weird. 'It's a nice place to work, really it is.'

'Good, good.' The chemist patted her shoulder and then turned to go back into his shop. 'But if you're ever worried by anything, my dear, or feel out of your depth, I'll be happy to give you any help or advice I can. After all, you're a long way from home and if *my* daughter was in trouble in your country, I like to think you or your parents would do your utmost to help her.'

'Sure we would, and thanks, I won't forget,' Summer said, turning away too. She walked down the village street towards the cafe, obscurely warmed and comforted by the little encounter. She felt she had made a friend and it was good to think that, even if Felix was at work, there was someone in the village she could turn to.

At the cafe, all was confusion, though even Summer could tell that it was organized confusion. The waitresses were moving the tables at the back of the room together, so that they formed long trestles for twenty-six people instead of being only able to seat four apiece. This meant that the coach party could sit in a group and be served at once, leaving the rest of the room for ordinary customers. Summer did not, this time, offer to lend a hand but went straight to her room and put on her swimsuit, then dragged T-shirt and cut-offs over it. She emerged on to the landing, towel in hand, to find a sleepy-eyed Fay just coming out of the bathroom.

'Hello, Summer – off for a swim? Hang on a tick and I'll join you.'

'That'ud be great,' Summer said gladly, swinging her towel whilst Fay rooted through her own chest of drawers for her costume. 'Do you know any good places for a swim? Felix showed me one, but it's a steep walk from here and I don't want to be late for work.'

'I know lots of places,' Fay said joyfully. 'Oh boy, I do love swimming! I'm going to enjoy the next couple of weeks and then when I get my G.C.S.E. results I shall know whether I've got resits or whether I can go ahead and start at sixth-form college next September. Once I know, whichever way it's gone, I suppose I'll have to start studying again in my spare time.'

'I know the feeling,' agreed Summer as they went side by side down the stairs. 'Are you going to college?'

'I hope so. I want to be a vet.'

'Gee! That takes some doing, back home.'

'And here. You can be a doctor easier. I'm very good at biology, and I'm all right at maths, but you really need chemistry and if I get that, it'll be by the skin of my teeth. I've taken ten G.C.S.E.s and I shall need three really good "A" levels or four not quite so good . . .'

The two heads, one glowing red, one dark, were close together, and the talk became technical. Summer walked through the cafe without taking in one single thing other than that the tables and chairs all seemed to have found their places, and she and Fay went blithely out into the summer morning, bent on enjoying their freedom and on exploring each other's desires and aspirations.

They did not stop talking until they started swimming and even then their voices echoed out over the water as they swopped anecdotes, experiences and school stories. It was fascinating for both of them to see how the other was getting educated and if Summer missed Felix it was fleetingly, and when she thought of him it was with careless affection. She had never had much time for guys, she had been too busy getting good grades at school and taking care of her poor, worrying mother, then Felix had come along and she had gotten interested and indeed fond of him. Now, with Fay's uncomplicated companionship, she felt things were really in perspective. Guys were good fun – Felix was the greatest – but there was still a lot to be said for a girl who was really rather like you yourself!

5

'Summer . . . and Fay, too . . . thank goodness!' Angela the calm, Angela the organized, was beginning to show signs of strain. Of all things, a shower of rain had started just as the big cream-and-red coach drew into the car park a little further down the road, which meant not only that the hikers on it bolted for shelter, but so did dozens of holidaymakers who just happened to be in Castlebridge at that particular time. Summer and Fay entered with a rush too, their towels over their heads, to find Angela besieged by hopeful would-be customers and by forty-six young people in brightly coloured shirts and shorts with every conceivable sort of rucksack, all clamouring to find their tables and eager to abandon their bags, as the notice above the door bade them, and sit themselves down.

There was an entrance to the cafe through the gift shop and in view of the additional tables which had been set up, the ordinary cafe entrance had been temporarily blocked. This, Fay had told Summer earlier, served two purposes. It meant that the holidaying students had to pass through the gift shop in order to claim their places, which meant that Beryl could relieve them of their bags and keep them in the back room behind the shop until their owners had finished their meals. That was convenient for the waitresses, who hated tripping over luggage as they hurried between the tables. It also meant that the students would have to pass the enticingly laden shelves with their novelties, their china shepherdesses and their souvenirs, before being able to eat. In theory, at least, more than half the young people would spend money in the gift shop before entering the cafe and that was nice for the Bloxhams, since their meal in the cafe was pre-booked and also pre-paid for, so meant no additional profit.

However, because of the rush, half the students, impatient with the delay due to the sheer number of customers, pushed their way straight through into the cafe and sat themselves down at the booked tables, dropping their bags on to the floor and effectively blocking the waitresses' way through. So the moment Angela set eyes on Summer and Fay her message was clear.

'Girls, don't worry about changing or anything just for a moment. Slip a pinny round you to give you an official look and grab a roll of cloakroom tickets. Pin one on to each bag and give the counterfoil to the owner, then carry the bags through and dump them behind the counter. Then, when you've cleared them all up, perhaps you can absolutely whiz upstairs and get into your waiting on things.'

'Glad to help,' Summer said, hurrying about her task, but she had barely dumped the first couple of bags behind the counter when Ozzie came through from the kitchen, looking horribly harassed.

'That won't do . . . health and safety rules . . .' he muttered, picking up a knapsack by its straps and coasting it along the floor towards Summer, who was standing by the counter with another bag held at the ready. 'Take them straight through to the back room behind the shop, there's a good girl. Got to have a clear passageway here, too.'

Accordingly Summer, laden as a Christmas tree with bags, made her way through into the gift shop – not easy, fighting against the stream of people trying to get into the cafe – and there, seeing that there was no one behind the counter since Mrs Shoggles and Jenny Platt were both serving customers from the freezers, she proceeded on her way round the counter and into the back room.

Beryl was there. What was more, Beryl was doing something very odd indeed with a dark-blue rucksack; she had it turned upside down and she appeared to be disembowelling it – at any rate a part of it hung down like a flapping tongue and Beryl's hand was disappearing into the inner recesses.

Summer saw what was happening before Beryl saw her, which was a lucky break because she was able to half turn in the doorway and to pretend that she was having difficulty in getting through it. When, puffing, she more or less burst into the back room, Beryl was pinning a cloakroom ticket on to the dark-blue bag – innocently upright once more – and glanced up briefly, before saying brusquely, 'Put them down here, Summer. Ta.'

Summer returned to the cafe in a thoughtful frame of mind. She had seen Beryl digging about inside that rucksack and was just grateful that she herself had been given no opportunity at any time to be alone with the bags so that when – if – the owners discovered they had been robbed, no enquiry could lead back to Summer herself.

During the course of that hectic lunchtime, Summer went backwards and forwards several times with various bags, but never again was Beryl doing anything even faintly suspicious. The girls rushed around, Mrs Shaw and Angela cooked and stewed and toasted and roasted, and at long last everyone was fed, the coach party began to disperse, and Summer waited, with a most unpleasant tingling feeling all down her spine, for trouble to come.

Trouble, however, did not occur. The holidaying students got their bags back, several of them wandered back into the gift shop to buy bits and pieces; wallets, purses and notecases were produced . . . and not one single person gave any indication that everything was not just as it should be. Indeed one scatty little French girl, with many Gallic exclamations, turned her haversack upside down all over the floor, went through the contents one by one, and finally decided that she had not got a suitable present for Maman, and that a china shepherdess would be just the thing.

She paid, so did the others, and at long, long last, they left. Even the ordinary customers, who had had quite a long wait for their meals, left. The room began to look less like a battlefield, the kitchen was no longer full of steam and – regrettably – swearing, and Summer felt the tensions coiled within her gradually ease and release their grip.

She glanced at her watch and was astonished to realize that it was nearly four o'clock; half her shift had gone and she was still on her feet. Felix would either be in Keswick searching for Nell or working at the garage. She guessed that in order to go with his boss he would have had to ask for some time off. Several times during the afternoon she had looked up at people hurrying along the sidewalk, half hoping one of them would be Felix, but it never was and of course she should not have expected to see him, knowing as she did that he was either working hard or far from Castlebridge.

'Take a break, Fay, Summer,' Angela said at last. 'There's a meal for you in the kitchen.'

The two of them went through and slumped into chairs. The cafe was no longer crowded but already people were coming in for afternoon tea and it was better that the waitresses took their break in the kitchen. Mrs Shaw, still red-faced but cheerful now that the worst was over, slapped egg and chips on to their plates and poured them the inevitable tea. Summer thought hopefully that she might grow to enjoy the nauseous brew since familiarity does not always breed contempt, but at least the tea was wet, which was good when you were as dry as she was.

Summer and Fay were alone for ten minutes and then Liz joined them and, shortly after that, Sandy came in. The four of them ate and drank with scarcely a word exchanged and then continued to sit limply in their chairs sipping tea, too exhausted to want to move until their twenty-minute break was up.

'Our turn now, angel-girls,' Angela said cheerfully, when the last of the tea had been drunk and applepie and custard had been devoured. 'My poor old plates! They're killing me.'

'Plates are feet,' Fay said kindly at Summer's astonished expression. 'Don't ask me why, because I haven't a clue. Come on, ducks, back to the scene of the crime!' Together, they went back to the cafe and back, of course, to the eager, thirsty customers.

'She wasn't there,' Felix said, as he and Summer sat side by side on the parapet of the bridge much later that night. The rain had cleared hours before but there were still clouds in the sky; occasionally a cloud drifted across the face of the moon and the countryside darkened for a moment but for most of the time the moonlight lit the scene almost as clearly as daylight would have done.

'Wasn't where? Did you get her address, then?' Summer had been so glad to see him back safe and sound that she had scarcely asked him what had happened to him, and she was also dying to tell him all about her afternoon. The mysterious behaviour of Beryl with the rucksacks was something which would, she felt, occupy them both for quite a long time!

'Yes, of course I got it. Well, I used some guile,' Felix admitted, grinning at her. He looked nice, Summer thought, with a lock of his dark hair dangling across his brow and that rueful, half-guilty smile on his mouth. 'I told Angela that Nell owed me a fiver and I wanted to look her up whilst I was in Keswick with Bob and see if I could get it back. She told me like a shot.'

'Why didn't you tell her the truth?' Summer found herself thinking of what the chemist had said earlier in the day. Nell was sly, he had said, she made up stories. Did Felix rather like her, nevertheless, and was that the real reason for chasing round after her like this? Could Felix not tell Angela the truth about Nell because he had been involved with her before she was sent packing? Was he still interested in her? Summer's stomach gave an aching lurch at the thought and she told herself not to be so stupid. He's a nice guy, she reminded herself desperately, but nothing special. Not that special. He's just . . . oh, he's Felix, and I like him better than I ever thought I could!

'Tell her the truth?' Felix echoed scornfully now. 'Hell, Summer, how can I tell anyone anything when I don't even know what the truth is? I'm uneasy, that's all. Or I was, rather.'

'You aren't now? But you said she wasn't there.'

'She surely was not, but her mom was. Her mom

asked me in for a cup of tea and scarcely stopped talking for twenty minutes,' Felix said a trifle ruefully. 'Said Nell gave notice because she didn't like the way Ozzie treated her. Apparently Nell's got a feller she's quite serious about, and the feller says he'll get her a much better job than she had in Castlebridge and then they'll get married and all that. Nell's mom obviously believed every word and was happy with the situation, so I feel better about it.'

'Felix,' Summer said, after a thoughtful pause. 'Just what did you think had happened to Nell?'

'Well . . . it's all mad, of course, but I did wonder if . . . Well, she was a great one for going off into the hills on her time off, and I did kinda wonder if she'd seen your Caliban and . . . well, and not run quite so fast.'

'Oh, but what about Ozzie saying they'd had a row? He wasn't worried.'

'No, he wouldn't be, a girl is just a waitress to Ozzie. But I could see Nell was just the sort of girl to get herself into some sort of trouble.'

'I don't get it,' Summer said rather crossly. 'Did you *like* Nell, Felix? Was she a friend of yours?'

'No, I can't say I liked her much, but I felt kinda sorry for her. She was a greedy, grabby sort of girl in a lot of ways, but she could be fun, too. Cheerful, bouncy, like that. I took her out twice, but she wanted someone to spend a lot of money on her, not someone to share a laugh and a bag of french fries. And once or twice I'd seen her with a guy who could possibly have been your Caliban. Tough, mean and scruffy, like you said. Not the sort of guy to get grabby and greedy with, if you get my meaning. So I thought . . .'

'I *see*,' Summer breathed, immensely relieved to realize that she spoke no more than the truth, for she did indeed see. Nell had a row with Ozzie, walked out of the place, might easily have gone up into the hills the way Felix said she liked to. Then she disappeared. Ozzie assumed she had gone home, but Felix, who was kind and cared about people, even about greedy, grabby girls like Nell, Felix worried that Nell might have fallen foul of Caliban and might not, as he put it, have run fast enough. 'But you're not worried now? Not since you spoke to Nell's mother?'

'Not at all worried. So we can forget one weird thing. What happened to you today? No more Calibans, I trust and hope?'

'Well, no, but . . .'

The story of the rucksacks was short and sweet, but it left Felix with that crease between his eyebrows again. He kicked himself away from the parapet however, and dropped lightly on to the road.

'Hell, it's a mystery and no mistake! Tell you what, Summer, what shift are you working tomorrow? The early? Eight until two? Great, then we'll meet after you've eaten, go for a swim and think some more. I'm sure there's something going on in that place, but I just can't imagine what!'

Next morning Summer woke again to blue skies and sunshine. She had written to her mother the evening before, giving her the temporary Castlebridge address, so her conscience was clear. If by some mischance Aunt Peggy got in touch with Mom then Mom would explain. Otherwise, Summer intended to ring her aunt in a week or so and tell her what had happened. Right now, she went down for the staff breakfast, sat next to Fay and chattered happily about her studies, her life, her holiday. She even told Fay about Aunt Peggy and the holiday-that-wasn't, but she had enough sense not to add that Aunt Peggy

79

would be returning to her home in a few days. She felt a bit mean in a way, but she was somehow quite certain that if Ozzie and his daughter knew she was only staying until the end of the week they would get rid of her right away. It made no sense to train a girl up just to see her leave. And anyway, Summer was not at all sure that she intended to turn meekly round and go back to Aunt Peggy's. How bored she would be there, how dull it would seem after her time in Castlebridge! No, she would telephone Aunt Peggy and explain, perhaps go over and spend a day with her, but she would not abandon her friends, her job and, above all, Felix, without a much better excuse than duty to a remote, never-before-met godmother!

Having made up her mind on that point she busied herself in the cafe and was totally unprepared when, halfway through the morning, the kitchen door was pushed open and a man staggered in, half hidden by the crate of bottles in his arms.

She could not see his face, could only see his hands and arms clutching the crate and his bandy legs below it, but she did not have to see anything else. The sneakers, one tied with string, would have given her the last clue to his identity, but the whole of her body seemed to know that behind the crate was Caliban.

Summer had not known before that legs really can turn to jelly, but hers did their best to do so. Her hands began to shake and all the little hairs on the back of her neck stiffened and stood upright, fear and revulsion fighting for supremacy. It was, it was! Hateful, terrorizing Caliban was actually within six feet of her . . . He would smash her face in . . .

Summer had been standing meekly by the cooker whilst Mrs Shaw piled her tray with hot buttered scones fresh out of the oven; now she took off in the direction of the cafe because that was the obvious escape route. She fled, slopping coffee and scattering scones, and not caring a bit what people thought until the swing doors had been passed and had swung closed and she was on her way across the floor, wishing she could continue straight on and leave the whole building far behind her.

Strangely enough, no one seemed to notice her wild flight. To be sure Liz followed her out and discreetly slipped on to the plate an erring scone, but other than that there was no outcry from the kitchen, no stocky male figure burst through the doors vowing vengeance. Indeed, no Mrs Shaw or Angela came after her, and Summer concluded, thankfully, that they merely thought her extra-keen to take her order through.

Liz, having delivered the scone, would have returned for her own order, but Summer detained her.

'Liz, hang on a minute . . . Who was that man who came into the kitchen just as I left?'

'The walking crate, you mean? That was the Samplex delivery man, he's often in and out. Ozzie's got another cafe, you know, much further off the beaten track than this one is, and so Samplex are ever so useful to him. Ozzie buys for us here and for his other place, and Samplex delivers to both. Sometimes Ozzie sends batches of scones or cases of soft drinks or whatever up with the Samplex man, when his other place is running short. Of course, the feller isn't supposed to take stuff, but he does it to oblige, so Ozzie puts a lot of business his way. Why do you ask?'

'I thought I'd seen him before . . . the Samplex man, I mean. Up in the hills.'

'Who, Dirty Dan? Never! I can't imagine him walking for pleasure!'

'Perhaps I was wrong. Why do you call him Dirty Dan, though?'

'Because he's a filthy little tyke, not that you could say anything rude about him in front of Nell. She fancied him, believe it or not!'

'Fancied him?' Summer said hollowly. This was a nightmare! Just when she and Felix had decided their fears were all imagination Caliban had turned up to make her, at any rate, think again! 'I didn't know she even knew him – let alone fancied him!'

'Course she knew him, we all do, you can't not, if you work here,' Liz said scornfully. 'You'll know him soon, you poor thing! Come on, back to work, those people at table seven are looking ever so hopefully at you!'

For the rest of the morning Summer worked in a daze. When she returned to the kitchen though she found to her relief that Caliban had been and gone. Piles of various foodstuffs testified to the fact. And very soon she found it possible to go into the kitchen without staring, wild-eyed, at the back door, without expecting it to crash open to reveal Caliban come to take vengeance.

Then, when she really did feel safe, when she was lulled by a false sense of security into humming gaily as she served her customers, a man came in through the gift-shop doorway.

Every nerve in her body told her that it was he before she swung round to face him, and this time there was no escape. He looked at her, his glance slithered past, indifferent, and then returned, sharpened and caught. He knew her! Without a shadow of a doubt he recognized her for the girl he had sworn at and chased that day on the hillside!

Summer half turned away, only to find Ozzie close behind her. But Caliban was making no move, no outcry, no fuss. He was walking across the cafe and sitting down at a table . . . it was actually one of hers . . . and picking up the menu and studying it . . .

It was unbelievable, because she knew he had recognized her. Summer went back into the kitchen, collected her order and carried it back to the cafe. Caliban looked up at her and actually jerked his head. Summer went towards him, stiffening her sinews, summoning up her blood, and generally doing Shakespearian things to engender courage in battle. She would not whimper and tremble and run – they were in a crowded cafe, he could scarcely hurt her here!

'Egg, sausage, beans and chips,' Caliban said, studying the menu. 'Mug of tea too, miss, not a cup, and a plate of bread and butter.' He looked up at her, his mean, hot little eyes searching. 'What's the matter? Have I seen you somewhere before?'

It was such an old line that Summer, despite her fear, found herself smiling. Her smile got broader and broader, so that she actually spluttered on a laugh.

'Yes, of course – in the kitchen, this morning,' she said bravely and, giggling, knew that she was close to hysteria. 'Why?'

His eyes had been fixed on hers almost hypnotically, but now their gaze dropped to the menu in his hand.

'Yes, 'course, that's it,' he muttered. 'And make the chips a double portion.'

'Would you like a drink before your meal or with it?' Summer said, almost delirious with relief. He had recognized her all right, but he did not realize that recognition had been mutual and for some reason that was enough to get him off her back!

'I'll have the tea at once, and a coke later,' Caliban said. He cast a quick glance back towards the kitchen where Ozzie still stood, measuring milkshake

83

syrup into a glass. Something about the look made Summer believe that Caliban was most anxious that Ozzie should not know there was anything, even enmity, between herself and the Samplex delivery man.

Still wildly relieved but extremely puzzled too, Summer made her way out of the cafe and back to the kitchen. She served the rest of the meal, did her duty by her other customers, and then, when two o'clock came round, went to her room and got into her bathing suit. It was an extremely hot day and she thought it would be both suitable and sensible to go swimming with Felix and then walk back to the cafe in her suit, to change for the evening. Perhaps they could go up the track to the quiet little beach they had visited last time; it was better than the public beach where she and Fay had bathed.

Only one other thing happened to disturb her peace of mind. As she went down to find Felix, she heard Liz and Sandy chatting as they cleared their tables and Liz was telling Sandy that Dirty Dan had asked her where Nell was.

'I'd probably have told him,' she said cheerfully, swabbing the glass tabletop with a checked cloth, 'but our Ozzie was in first. Day off, he told him, cool as you please, and Dan just grunted and went out. Odd, isn't it? But if Dirty Dan really was getting keen on Nell then he'd be liable to land Ozzie one for sacking her, perhaps.'

And Summer, making her way out of the cafe to meet Felix, could only agree with Liz that it was indeed odd!

'Who said curiouser and curiouser?' Felix demanded when Summer had related the story of her nerve-racking day. 'So Caliban's the Samplex man, is he? I suspected as much. Well, I didn't know he was a delivery man, I just thought he was that nasty piece of work I'd seen Nell sloping off with. So now what've we got?' The two of them were lying in shallow water quite near the shore with just their heads above the surface. Felix counted points off on his fingers. 'One, Beryl goes through customers' rucksacks. Two, Caliban knew you but didn't try to break your neck, despite previous promises to do just that. Three, Caliban and Nell were involved in some way and Ozzie lied about her leaving the place. Four . . . well, there isn't a four.'

'Yes there is,' Summer said. 'Four is that you were right when you said Caliban wasn't cross because I was trespassing, or because I saw something I shouldn't. He was cross because I saw *him*, not for any other reason. Well, at least, I think that must be so, otherwise he wouldn't be so pleased with himself when he thought I didn't recognize him though he knew he knew me.' Summer paused, trying to unravel this tortuous sentence. 'If you see what I mean,' she finished doubtfully.

'Actually, I do. So it wasn't the cards that mattered.' Felix flicked wet hair off his face, then smoothed it flat with the palms of his hands. 'At one point I thought the cards might be significant . . .'

Summer sat up with a splash. In the back of her mind all this time she had been thinking about those cards and now, suddenly, she remembered the dream, which had not been just a dream at all.

'Felix, I've got it! It sounds insane, but listen! The cards Caliban had spread out on the rock weren't cards at all, they were little packets of sugar! They've got coloured photographs on the front, that's why I thought they were cards, and the reason I know they weren't is because I found one of them, an empty one, in the top drawer of my dressing table. I suppose Nell left it there.'

'*Sugar* packets? Summer, are you sure? Do you still have the empty one you found?'

'No, of course not, it was empty so I chucked it . . .' Summer remembered the scene, the quiet little room, the slanting sunshine, the absence of a waste-paper basket. 'Jeez, it's still in my room at the cafe!'

'Was there anything about it that was out of the ordinary? Special in some way?'

Summer thought, then reluctantly shook her head. 'No, I guess not. It was just empty. And the ones Caliban was messing about with . . .' She closed her eyes tightly, so tightly that she saw coloured lights whirling against her eyelids. She forced herself to concentrate, to remember, and saw the little scene again: Caliban's dark, hirsute hands, the little packets, the half-completed movement he had been making as she rounded the big boulder . . . 'Oh, Felix, I think . . . I think most of the sugar packets Caliban had were empty too; but some were full. Felix, I think Caliban was filling them up from a squarish box.'

'You guessing, honey?'

Summer thought again, then nodded, unsmiling. 'Reckon I am, but that doesn't mean to say I'm wrong! For some reason Caliban was taking sugar out of those little packets and putting something else in. Felix, I think he's smug druggling!'

'Smug druggling?' Felix snorted with laughter and then became deadly serious. 'That's all very well but where does he get the stuff from and where does he take it and why should he be doing it on top of a mountain?'

'I don't *know* . . . but surely we can find out? All we need is a bit of proof and then we can go to the police and I can stop worrying that Caliban will come

86

sneaking into my room some dark night and strangle me with his bare hands.'

Until she said it, Summer had not fully realized that was how she felt, but once the words had been uttered, she knew she would not sleep soundly in her bed until Caliban was either behind bars or proved innocent. If he was involved in some sort of drug smuggling, and it looked very like it to Summer, then she had seen him working with the drug and her life would not be worth a cent.

The same thought must have occurred to Felix for his hands came out of the water and held hers tightly for a moment.

'You're right . . . I should have stayed, seen Nell! We could go to the cops right now, of course, tell them what we suspect, but I agree it's a pretty thin tale, all our word against his. You think he carries the stuff in his van, of course, disguised as packets of sugar.'

'I suppose so. I wonder where he gets them?'

'From the cafe, of course. That's why Beryl pokes around in rucksacks. She gets the smuggled stuff out and Caliban takes it to a city somewhere, and sells it on.'

'They they're *all* in it? Ozzie and Beryl too? Holy cow!'

'Well, I don't know, it could have been just Nell and Caliban, but if Beryl was involved it would explain the business over the rucksacks. Look, when does Caliban come to you again?'

'Not tomorrow,' Summer said. 'Probably the day after. Why? What are you thinking of doing?'

'Taking a look in his van whilst he's having a meal,' Felix said grimly. 'Find out when the next delivery's due, there's a good girl, and we'll act on it.'

'Right.' Summer got to her knees and floated

herself off the sandbank they were lying on and into deeper water. 'You will be careful though, won't you, Felix? I think Caliban's quite dangerous and probably even Ozzie could be, if he was cornered. They say cornered rats are dangerous, you know.'

'I'll be careful. The trouble is, you've worried me, talking about Caliban. Does your door have a good lock on it? Not that I think you're in any danger really, but . . .'

'My door has a good little bolt and I'll use it tonight,' Summer promised, with a strong shudder. 'I'm not heroine material, Felix. No one is keener to see me safe than I am! Are you coming back to the cafe with me now, to have some supper? I wouldn't mind a bit of moral support, if you've got any to spare.'

'That's a good idea,' Felix said, rising, dripping, from the water. Summer followed suit and they waded ashore and towelled themselves dry. 'I think I might have a word with our friendly local cop even if we don't find proof too soon. It wouldn't hurt and it might save a lot of explanations later.'

Presently, dried and with their towels slung round their necks, the two of them made their way back to the cafe. The sun was wending its way down the sky now, gilding the pine trees, the village roof-tops and the humped purple of the high hills. Felix would have gone straight into the cafe through the double doors but Summer held him back.

'Say, Felix, have a heart. You've got jeans but I'm still in my bathers! Come round the back and you can wait in the kitchen whilst I change, then we can eat together.'

'Sure,' Felix agreed and together they walked up the side alley and through the gap by the five-barred gate, into the yard. A big van was parked there and

Summer was about to pass it when she glanced at the name on the side and froze, a hand going to her mouth.

'Felix, that's the Samplex van. Caliban must be inside the cafe having a meal! Oh darn it, I'm scared!'

89

6

'Hi, Summer, have a good swim?'

Angela, coming through the swing doors into the cafe with a tray of used crockery, greeted the younger girl cheerfully, and Summer had to make a real effort to answer in a similar vein.

'Great, thanks! I thought I'd come in for a meal, if that's all right.'

'Yes, fine. You go up and change and we'll eat together, you, me and Liz. It's quiet this evening, not too much doing.'

Nonchalantly, as if it did not matter at all, Summer strolled towards the cafe and peered in. She could see several customers, Caliban amongst them, but it was impossible to see what stage his meal had reached, and Felix had asked her to find out. She moved back into the kitchen just as Liz came through the doors. Trying for a natural tone, Summer said: 'I see Dirty Dan's dining with us. Nearly finished, has he?'

'Barely started,' Liz said, grinning. 'He likes his stomach well lined before a journey, does Dan.'

It would have to be sufficient. Summer gave a simulated start, looked all round the kitchen, and then headed for the back door.

'Must have dropped my towel in the yard. Shan't be a moment.'

Outside, she moved round the van, out of range of the kitchen windows. Felix lurked there. 'This will be the best chance we're likely to get to have a snoop round his van,' he had said impressively ten minutes earlier, when they had realized that the van doors, though almost closed, were most definitely not locked. 'Go in, honey, and make sure he isn't about to come out – I don't fancy being caught in the act by Caliban. If he looks set for ten minutes or so then I'll risk it and take a peep. You can stand guard for me.'

So now, as she came round the corner, Felix's mobile brows shot up. Summer, swallowing nervously, nodded.

'He's eating. Liz says he's barely started. Felix, don't you think . . .'

But Felix was not wasting time in thought, he was acting. He swung himself up on the rear fender and opened the door just wide enough to admit him. Safely inside the van, he turned and addressed Summer sternly before vanishing into the interior.

'Go back, honey, and act natural, but keep an eye open. If you see him, make some excuse . . . shout, warn me somehow. Detain him if you can. Go on!'

There was nothing for it, she would have to obey him. Summer turned and went back in through the door, brandishing her towel which Felix had been holding.

'Got it! Say, if I tied it round my waist do you think the customers would be fooled into thinking I was respectable? Then I could give you a hand with the orders, get it cleared up quicker. I'm starved, I wouldn't say no to eating . . .'

Behind her, in the yard, she heard a bang and then the tinny roar of an engine starting up. For the life of her she could not hide her shock, nor the way her head turned towards the sound. She went over to the back door, telling herself that there must have been another vehicle in the yard – Caliban could not possibly be driving his van. Perhaps Felix had decided it would be safer to steal the vehicle and search it at his leisure someplace else.

She looked out of the kitchen window and hope died; Caliban was manoeuvring the heavy van in a turn. She could see his muscles bulging as he wrenched at the wheel, his brows scowling with the effort, and then he had got it lined up with the open gate and was driving it off . . . with Felix inside! As the van turned, Summer could see the back doors, firmly closed!

For a moment she was too dazed and terrified to speak. Felix was a prisoner, and it was all her fault! She had promised to raise the alarm, hold Caliban up for a few vital seconds while Felix climbed down from his high perch, and instead she had stood in the kitchen talking inanely whilst Felix's life was put at risk!

But how had he done it? How had the Samplex driver got out of the cafe and round into the yard so quickly and without coming through the kitchen? He had gone out the front way, of course, like a customer, and must have run down the side alley, slammed the van doors and vaulted into the driving seat in one movement, almost.

Angela, beside her, was staring out as well, looking puzzled.

'Hey, Liz, Dirty Dan's just left! I thought he'd still be chomping through his first course whilst we were waiting for our break!'

'He had a phone call,' Liz said laconically, cutting bread and sliding each slice as it was made into the toaster. 'Someone must have said they'd ring him here, on the public phone, because the moment it rang he was up and across to it. Then he just scarpered – no warning, didn't even pay for his tea.'

'Funny bloke.' Angela, losing interest, turned away from the window. 'Well, as soon as you've served your customers, Lizzie, we'll have our break. I fancy tomatoes on toast. How about you two?'

'Sure,' Summer said. Her mind was sick; now racing, now faltering. What on earth should she do? Caliban would open the van doors and find Felix . . . He might kill him!

'Summer? Is anything the matter? You've gone ever so white, girl.' Angela's voice was concerned and kindly but suddenly it felt to Summer as though everyone in any way connected with the cafe or the gift shop could be an enemy. Suppose she told Angela and Angela told Ozzie or Beryl? First they would make sure, somehow, that Caliban was warned of his stowaway and then they would silence her, Summer. She must get to the police station somehow and tell them what had happened. They could radio ahead, get the Samplex van stopped, release Felix together with any information his snooping had managed to bring forth.

She took two steps towards the back door, then remembered her swimsuit. A real fool she would look running to the police station in her present garment – someone would notice and alert Ozzie, or possibly Angela would think she had gone off her head and try to detain her. What on earth was she going to do? Who would help her rescue Felix?

As if in answer to her unspoken prayer, she heard a voice in her head. *If you're ever worried by anything, my dear, or feel out of your depth, I'll be happy to give you any help or advice I can.*

The words were the chemist's, and the chemist was right next door to the gift shop, not a mile away like the police station! What was more, she could slip jeans and a T-shirt on and pretend to have a headache and go straight over there. He was open, still, but even if he had closed there was a bell one could ring; he was down in an instant, she had heard someone saying so in the cafe only the other day. She could ask for aspirin and then tell him what had happened, beg for his help.

The idea was obviously heaven-sent. Telling the girls that she would not be a moment, Summer rushed up to her room and came down almost at once, respectably dressed once more.

'I'm just going to pop over to the chemist before we eat,' she heard her voice telling Angela in a calm, sensible sort of tone. 'There's something I need . . . shan't be long.'

She escaped out of the back door and into the cool evening air. She hurried down the side alley and round into the road, passing the cafe and gift shop without a glance or, indeed, a thought. She must get help for Felix before the worst happened!

The chemist's shop was not exactly open, but he was in there, working in the little dispensary behind the counter. The door was shut but, when she tried it, it swung open easily. The chemist heard her and popped his head out.

'Is that you, Mrs Rivers? I shan't be a moment, I'm just finishing the cough mixture.'

'No, it's me,' Summer said awkwardly, even as she saw recognition and a smile dawn on the chemist's face. 'I'm sorry to disturb you, but I remembered what you said and . . . and . . .'

'Come into the dispensary, my dear,' the chemist said, seeing her hesitation. 'I'm just making up a prescription; you can talk to me whilst I work.'

Summer followed him into the small room, but

she had barely begun to speak when the door opened to admit a stout woman with grey hair pulled into a knot on the back of her head.

'Mr Sanderson? Is me cough medicine ready? And me tablets?'

'Be with you in a tick, Mrs Rivers. Just got to count out the last few antibiotic tablets then I'll bring it out to you.'

He went into the shop and gave Mrs Rivers her prescription, then hurried her out again into the street and turned back, a hand on the door.

'Is it confidential, my dear? I noticed you stopped speaking when Mrs Rivers came in.'

'Well, yes. Yes, it is,' Summer decided. Mr Sanderson nodded and turned the key in the lock. Then he returned to the back room, which contained his phials and bottles and jars.

'Sit down. The tall stools are quite comfortable if you're only on them for ten minutes or so,' Mr Sanderson said. 'You look excited and little apprehensive. Tell me what's worrying you.'

Now that she was actually being asked for her story, Summer found herself daunted by its sheer length and complexity. Where should she start? At the beginning, when she first saw Caliban up in the hills? Or now, with Felix being carried off? It was a difficult decision!

'It's Felix. He got into the Samplex van and the chap came out and drove off! If he catches Felix . . .'

The chemist's brows rose.

'Well, and I've always thought Felix such a sensible fellow! What ever made him decide to get into the van in the first place?'

Summer sighed. Of course she might have guessed that no one, not even an intelligent and sensible guy like Mr Sanderson, would be able to understand her predicament and, indeed, Felix's, without being told the whole story. Trying to speak clearly and concisely, she began.

'Well, sir, it was like this. I was coming to Castlebridge for a few days . . .'

She must have told the story quite well, for Mr Sanderson only interrupted her once and that was when she first mentioned the Samplex delivery man. Then he interrupted her not because he was surprised at Caliban's forceful reaction to her presence, but to ask on which day the encounter had taken place.

'Day? Why, Saturday, I guess,' Summer said. 'Last Saturday. Is it important?'

'Indeed it is, but never mind it for now. Go on.'

Summer went on. She told Mr Sanderson everything, including the story of the dreams and her realization that the cards Caliban had been playing with had not been cards at all, but sugar packets.

'Only we had no proof, you see,' she finished, having worked her way solidly through the whole story. 'And we knew we needed proof before anyone would believe us. So Felix got into the van to see if he could find some sugar packets, and I was supposed to warn him if I saw the driver. Only the driver got a phone call . . .'

'A phone call? From whom?'

Summer shrugged. 'I don't know. Does it matter? The point is the driver came running round the side of the cafe and jumped into the van and drove off before I could warn Felix and he's . . . he's in there. When that guy opens the door he's bound to see Felix and know he's been sussed.'

'I see. Yes, I do see. My dear, you'll have to tell your story again. Do you mind very much? Because otherwise I may have difficulty in convincing people myself.'

'No, I don't mind.' Summer slid off her stool. 'Shall we go now? I do think we should hurry, I dread Felix being discovered.'

'We're not going anywhere. Stay there, whilst I make a call.'

Summer relaxed for a moment. Thank heaven, he had believed her. Now he was calling the cops and very soon Felix would be safe! She heard Mr Sanderson returning, other footsteps, and then he came back into the dispensary. He was smiling.

'Here we are, my dear. Now start right at the beginning, if you don't mind . . .'

Behind him came Ozzie Bloxham, and by his side, Beryl!

When someone slammed the van doors shut, Felix thought crossly that he had been the victim of young-sters mucking about with the vehicle. Summer, however, was a good kid and reliable. She would see what had happened and hurry over to release him.

Then the engine started and, with a jolt of pure dismay, he felt the heavy van swing round, ponder-ously but definitely, and begin to move along the cobbled alley.

For a moment, Felix was too busy keeping his feet to wonder what had gone wrong. All around him Caliban's wares were piled up, boxed or bottled or bagged, and though the load was presumably secure, Felix himself was not. As the van gathered speed he was thrown from one side of the vehicle to the other, bruising himself considerably against sharp corners until he managed to wedge himself between two packing cases where he had leisure, for a moment, to consider his situation.

It was not good. As yet he had not managed to search for some sign that drugs were being conveyed in the van disguised as something else, but he had little doubt that Caliban was up to something shady and would resent finding a stowaway aboard his truck. If I do find drugs, Felix told himself ruefully, the guy is going to be pretty mad – he'll probably try to kill me.

On the other hand, Caliban was unlikely to guess that Felix was in the truck and that would give Felix the advantage of surprise, if he wasn't first thrown across the vehicle and knocked unconscious!

The van cornered at speed and Felix, on the left-hand side of the vehicle with his back to the bodywork, found himself abruptly on the right-hand side of it with his nose in violent collision with the panelling. This, he told himself with watering eyes, was liable to be a painful and depressing journey – he must take a hold of himself and wedge himself in somehow.

But for what felt like a lifetime, although it may well have been only an hour, Felix continued to be thrown painfully from one side of the truck to the other. Caliban, surely the world's lousiest driver, Felix thought vengefully, continued to hurl his vehicle along the narrow lanes of the Lake District at a suicidal pace, giving no thought to others, least of all to his unhappy passenger.

Finally, however, the van miraculously steadied; Caliban had arrived at a motorway, Felix guessed. After a ten-minute break to lick his wounds, Felix got cautiously to his feet and approached the nearest packing cases. It was dim in the van but not dark – a roof-light running the length of the body saw to that. Kneeling, Felix examined box after box and case after case until he found the one he was after. *Single-portion sugar packets*, the legend on the box read. *Best cane sugar; souvenir pictorial.*

Felix got out his penknife to lift the staples which held the lid in place, then put it away again. This box had obviously been opened, and recently, too. The staples were not fastened. Inside, as advertised, the sugar packets were packed in dozens. Felix fumbled a handful out and examined them. Close inspection showed that out of the six in his hand, two had been sealed with less than precision. He slit one open, tipped the contents into the palm of his hand and tasted with the tip of his tongue. Granulated sugar. He opened one which looked properly and efficiently sealed. As soon as he poured some of the contents on to his hand he could feel the difference: not rough and gritty, like sugar, but smoother, more like cornflour. He wet his finger and licked it, half hoping that it would prove innocuously sweet.

It was most definitely not sugar.

Felix gave a long sigh. Then, as carefully as possible when speeding along a motorway locked in the back of a badly driven truck, he repacked the boxes, keeping only four of the little packets – two sugar, two not. He pushed the staples home with his thumb, then sat back and thought, the sugar packets safe in his jeans pocket.

The ill-sealed packets containing sugar were undoubtedly the ones Caliban had been playing with when Summer had seen him up on the hillside last Saturday. He must have been given them by Nell, or possibly he had extracted them from the full box himself, and then he had carried them, and a packet of sugar, up into the hills where he had painstakingly unglued them, tipped out their contents, replaced it with sugar and sealed them up again. The drug – if it was a drug – which he had taken would undoubtedly be here somewhere, well hidden, so that he could sell it for his own profit when he reached his destination.

Felix wondered what would happen to Caliban if the users ever discovered they had been cheated, but he thought the delivery man was probably safe enough. He was selling to a pusher, he must be, and the pusher himself was unlikely to take the drug, he was merely selling it on. The man in the street who was cheated would never be believed . . . would probably end up dead if he made a fuss. In a way, Felix mused, you could almost say Caliban was a public benefactor, if only he had simply thrown the drug away. But Felix was not fool enough to believe that for one minute. No, Caliban would be selling it all right.

Felix leaned back against the nearest crate and tried to relax; he must conserve his energies for what he would do to the unsuspecting Caliban when the delivery man opened the van's double doors.

'Now, my dear.' Mr Sanderson was smiling, leading Ozzie and Beryl into the dispensary and addressing Summer as though he had not listened to a word she had just said. 'If you wouldn't mind repeating what you've just told me to these good people? I'm sure, you see, that you are mistaken in a lot of your conclusions, and I can best prove it to you this way. Start with meeting the Samplex delivery driver up in the hills above Castlebridge, would you?'

So calmly and authoritatively did he speak that for a moment Summer was almost deceived into believing that he truly meant what he said and was trying to help her. But then she glanced at Beryl and saw, in the older girl's expression, the gloating, cruel amusement of one who sees another in a trap from which there can be no escape.

'Tell . . . certainly not!' she said firmly. 'Please let me go at once, Mr Sanderson. Angela knows I'm here, she'll come across if I don't go back pretty soon.'

'No, my dear, you mustn't underestimate me. Angela thinks you made an excuse to come over here, but really you've gone off with young Felix. I told her it was probably so and she was immediately relieved and by now has probably gone off to bed.'

'Well, Felix knows! He knows the Bloxhams are mixed up in all this, he knows Beryl takes stuff out of the rucksacks . . .' She stopped as Beryl stepped forward, hand raised threateningly. 'What does it matter what I say? We all know the truth – all in this room that is, and Felix.'

'Ah, Felix. If you think, my dear child, that Felix will survive an encounter with the people on whom the driver is calling, you must be extremely optimistic! Felix is but one young man. The people who await the driver's arrival with eagerness are many. Your young friend probably imagines that he will be up against one enemy.' Mr Sanderson chuckled, and Beryl and Ozzie both grinned sycophantically. 'But in fact, he will step right into a reception committee. I have already taken the precaution of ringing Glasgow and warning friends there of his impending arrival.'

Summer felt sick; she had meant to save Felix, but now it seemed she had plunged him into even deeper trouble. As deep, almost, as the trouble which she herself was facing.

'All right,' she said, trying to speak steadily and almost succeeding. 'All right, I shan't get much help from Felix tonight, but you can't keep me here for ever! Sooner or later you've got to let me go and then I'll go straight to the cops and tell them everything I know!'

'I'm sure you would,' the chemist said. He sounded almost regretful. 'That's why you won't be allowed to see them, my dear. But let's not speak of that. I've asked you to repeat to my friends here what you've already told me. What's the harm in that?'

'What's the good?' countered Summer, whilst her heart hammered and her palms grew sticky. 'We know what you've been doing, all of you, and Felix and I went down to the police station this evening to tell someone all about his suspicions. He said it would save time later, when we had all our proof.'

She saw by the faces around her that she had frightened them, made them think again, but Beryl suddenly pushed her face forward and spoke, her voice shrill and triumphant.

'You're a liar, Summer! No way did you go down to the station today! You was in swimming things . . . I saw you cross the pavement in front of the shop and you was in a swimsuit. Then you went round the back and it wasn't long before the van drove out. You never went to the police in your cozzie!'

Summer's heart sank but she hoped her face remained stony, indifferent.

'Please yourself what you believe,' she said. 'I'm leaving.'

She moved across the dispensary and felt her wrists seized from behind. She kicked and struggled, but with three to one against her she did not really have much chance. In two minutes her wrists were tied and Sanderson was threatening her with having her ankles tied too and, what was worse, with being silenced more permanently.

'You'll either tell your story to my friends or I'll chloroform you,' he said matter of factly. 'Know this smell?'

Sickeningly familiar, reminding Summer of childhood visits to the dentist and to casualty units, the smell crept across the room when he unstoppered the bottle. He waved a pad of lint near the opening and Summer was not the only one affected. Beryl coughed and went pale.

'Hey, Uncle Ned, don't wave that stuff about,' she complained. 'She'll talk.'

Summer looked from face to face. After all, what did it matter if she told what she knew? Mr Sanderson had already heard her story. Grudgingly, and as slowly as she dared, she began her tale again.

'So that little swine was double-crossing us,' Beryl said furiously, when Summer's voice had faded into silence. 'Taking some of the sugar packets and emptying them and then filling them up with something else – sugar, I suppose – and passing them off to our people as the real thing. You'd have thought he got enough for ferrying the stuff without having to sell it on his own account.'

'I fancy that was less the driver than that young Nell,' Sanderson said, rubbing his chin. 'Once she began to suspect she'll have wanted a piece of the action, and I daresay the driver wanted to keep his share for himself. Besides, I doubt very much if Dan had the brains to think of it. No, that'll be Nell. We'll have to put a stop to her.'

There was enough venom in the cultured voice to send an extra shiver down Summer's back, and she was not short of shivers on her own account. The situation could not turn much nastier, she thought desperately. They had settled Felix, or would be settling him when he arrived at the van's destination, and they had caught her . . . She dared not ask herself what they intended to do with her. So far Sanderson's only real threat to her had been to prevent her from seeing the cops, but her imagination winced away from the method by which he might stop that happening. Surely he did not mean to murder her?

Her speculations were cut short, perhaps fortunately, by Beryl's voice rising with indignation.

'But Nell didn't *know* anything, you know she didn't! She told Dad she knew there was something fishy going on after she'd spied on me and seen me taking the raw stuff out of the blue rucksacks, but she was barking up the wrong tree – she thought we were in cahoots with a load of half-baked students and when her "discreet questioning", as she put it, brought nothing but blank stares, she tackled Dad and got sacked. That isn't *knowing* anything!'

'She put two and two together, she wasn't unintelligent,' Sanderson said rather wearily. 'As it is, she's fairly wise to what goes on this end but she knows nothing about the Marseilles business. We'll warn them, get them to divert the buses for a few weeks until we've sorted Nell out, and then we'll start up again.'

'And in the meantime, what do we do about the Yank?' Beryl did not deign to look at Summer as she spoke. 'She knows the lot!'

'Yes, she does. Which is a great pity. However, you two had better go and behave normally in the cafe otherwise you'll be asked questions and that would never do. I'll deal with our transatlantic guest.'

Ozzie Bloxham looked uneasy but turned at once to leave the dispensary. Beryl, however, who Summer knew well was no friend of hers, lingered.

'What'll you *do*, Uncle Ned? You won't actually . . . Well, you won't do anything to bring the police down on us?'

'I shall do nothing so unwise,' Mr Sanderson said soothingly. 'Now off with you, my dear, and leave me and the girl to work out her destiny.'

Beryl left. Summer heard her go, not across the hop but out through a door in the back. No doubt she would be able to slide in through a back door in the gift shop and no one would ever connect her with the chemist – indeed, I did not do so myself, Summer remembered ruefully.

But Mr Sanderson was moving around his dispensary and presently he went out, locking the door behind him, and Summer could hear him climbing the stairs to his flat. She got up and moved across to the door, but of course he had locked it securely. Then she glanced at the tiny frosted glass window. If she had enough time she might be able to scramble on to the wide working surface beneath the window and lift the latch, even with her hands tied, though she would have to knock aside a lot of bottles and things in order to do so and she might make quite a lot of noise.

But it was no use even attempting it; already she could hear the chemist's footsteps on the stairs and all too soon the lock clicked, the handle turned, and his smiling, urbane face appeared in the doorway. He had a bottle in one hand, and a glass.

'Now, my dear, you and I are going to have a little party!' He poured from the bottle into the glass and Summer saw that it was whisky, or at least it said so on the label. He came towards her, still smiling. 'Can you take the glass, or shall I hold it to your lips for you? Just a little nip to keep out the cold, because we're going for a ride in my car presently.'

There was more than a little nip in the glass, it was over half full. Summer went as if to take it and knocked it all over the floor. The glass did not break but the spirit went everywhere.

Mr Sanderson tutted and bent to pick up the glass.

'Now come along, don't be foolish! A drink will calm our nerves.'

'Drink it yourself,' Summer panted, thoroughly scared. 'You can't make me drink it!'

She thought, naturally enough, that the chemist would scorn this suggestion but he poured himself a hefty measure and tossed it off in one swallow. Then he carefully refilled the glass.

'See, it's perfectly good, despite being a blend! Do join me, my dear! I'm not trying to make you drunk, because I want you to walk with me out to my car. I'm just trying to make things a bit easier for you.'

'Oh, are you,' Summer said, white-faced. 'Well, you can forget it! I'm not drinking anything and if you try to make me I'll scream the place down.'

This proved to be a foolish boast for without more ado Mr Sanderson picked up a wad of lint and pushed it into her mouth, securing the most unpleasant gag with a length of bandage whilst Summer flailed helplessly with her tightly bound wrists.

'There! Now you can shout all you like,' Mr Sanderson said breathlessly, stepping back to admire his handiwork. 'Not that it worries me if you do shout,' he added, and the very fact that he was so obviously rattled by the threat cheered Summer. It was a nuisance that she had told the man she would scream, she should have just gone ahead and done it, but although Sanderson pretended to be so suave and in control, it was clear that in fact he was no such thing. If she was quick and careful she might yet turn things to her advantage.

Having bound and gagged her, Sanderson then pushed the bottle of whisky into his jacket pocket and caught hold of Summer's arm.

'Come along now. No fuss, or I'll be forced to hurt you, and I don't want to do that.'

Summer walked out of the dispensary with alacrity and didn't protest about leaving the building and crossing the back yard towards the car. She had decided to make her next fight in the open, but a quick glance round the yard showed her that this was unlikely to be seen by anyone other than Mr Sanderson himself. It was a small yard, surrounded by tumbledown outbuildings, and the big gate opened into the same alley as that which serviced the cafe and gift shop. Even so, she refused to get into the car, and then wished she had not. Mr Sanderson suddenly punched her in the stomach and whilst she was bent over, trying to whoop air into her empty lungs, he simply forced her into the back seat of the car, locked the door, and climbed into the driver's seat.

The engine whirred into life and Sanderson drove out of the yard, down the alley, and turned left on to the road. It was dark, the sky overhead ablaze with stars, the moon a gleaming crescent, young and hopeful. Summer, jolting helplessly along in the car, wondered where he was taking her and what he would do when they got to their destination. She hoped he was going to lock her up somewhere for a few hours, but she did not really believe it. She believed, in her heart, that he would try to kill her.

7

In the back of the Samplex van Felix gritted his teeth
and endured as the journey went on and on. Once
they stopped, and he heard the tank being filled with
gas. Once he suspected they parked whilst Caliban
had a drink and probably relieved himself, but other
than that the journey continued for three hours and
for three hours Felix wondered what he should do
when the doors opened.

Darkness crept down though, which made things
easier; he might even manage to sneak out of the van
without a confrontation with his enemy. Then, with
the evidence in his pocket, he had only to get himself
to the nearest police station to find immediate help.

For a good deal of the three hours though, Felix
worried about Summer. She was just the sort of girl
he found easiest to like – pretty, rather shy and not
over-confident, and the thought of her in some
dreadful danger had all his hackles up in a moment.
As soon as the van had started to move he guessed
that something had gone badly wrong with their
plan; Summer had scarcely had time to regain the
kitchen, let alone to realize Caliban was leaving.
Indeed, he found himself devoutly wishing that she
might remain in ignorance or assume he had followed
the van, himself a free agent, rather than guess the
truth.

For unless he was very wide of the mark, Summer would not see him carried off a captive without trying to do something about it, and the more Felix thought the more convinced he became that the pair of them had uncovered a rich – and therefore dangerous – drug-smuggling racket. If Summer went straight to the police and then kept clear of the cafe all might be well, but if the people running the racket realized she was wise to them . . . Felix tried not to think what they might do. They would not dare allow her to go free, he was sure of it. Groaning, he punched the side of the van with his fists. He was powerless to help her, powerless to warn her to do nothing, that action could well endanger them both. All he could do was get free as quickly as possible, and get back to Castlebridge.

The van was by no means new and through one of the many gaps in the bodywork Felix saw that it was not pitch dark. Having so long to consider, he now decided that when the van stopped he would get as near to the opening as possible, either hit Caliban with something heavy and make his escape before anyone could follow, or just cut and run. If the delivery man had a reception committee waiting then he would have to take a chance on getting away in the dark before anyone was aware of his presence. So Felix waited grimly for the moment of truth to arrive.

It came. For a while Felix had been aware that the van was being driven slowly and a good deal more carefully and guessed they had arrived in a large town or city. Then the van turned a very sharp corner, the glare of sodium lighting disappeared, and the vehicle drew to a halt.

For a moment there was nothing, no sound at all, then Felix heard the seat creak as Caliban moved, probably stretched and then yawned jaw-crackingly.

Then the door of the cab opened and the vehicle swayed as the man climbed down.

Desperately listening, Felix waited. He had armed himself, at the last minute, with a mammoth catering tin of baked beans. Now he stood to one side in the dark, knowing that the man was very unlikely to open both doors, hoping desperately that this was Caliban's private and illegal stop, so he would put his head to the right to find his doctored packets, rather than to the left, where the big boxes of supplies stood.

The door creaked open and Caliban's head and shoulders appeared inside the van. Just as Felix had hoped, he was reaching out for the boxes of sugar.

Felix raised the tin. He could not slip out of the doorway and run with Caliban's heavy torso completely blocking his path. It would have to be a touch of violence.

The movement must have caught Caliban's eye, however. He gave a startled grunt and moved just as the beans came crashing down. The tin caught him only a glancing blow, but it was enough. He lurched sideways and Felix jumped down just as someone crossed the yard towards them.

'Dan? Have you got the stuff, lad?'

Caliban, no doubt seeing stars, started to gurgle but Felix did not wait to meet the newcomer. He jumped clear over his enemy's crouching figure and made for the entrance to the yard. Because he had been in the dark for so long he could see his adversaries quite plainly, one of whom had come from the lighted building behind him. Caliban, who had been driving with headlights on, was still unable to see anything much. However, he could shout. Appalling roars split the air and Felix was almost relieved to hear Caliban shouting, 'Follow him, you fools! If it's the law, we're in trouble!'

Having made for the entrance, Felix promptly doubled back on himself and instead of making for the lights of a main road, he went with speed but no noise into another small entrance which led back into the yard he had just left. Crouching behind a pile of empty boxes, he watched as the men, with Caliban game but groaning, disappeared like hounds after a fox through the big double doors. Would they go far enough for him to get away unseen, or would they reach the lighted road and give up, or worse, realize they had been tricked?

Felix listened, but there was no sound of the men returning. He was actually out of hiding and halfway to the van when a figure lurched round the corner. Caliban. This time he looked straight across at Felix.

Afterwards, Felix realized why he had not been challenged. Caliban knew – or thought he knew – that his uninvited passenger was being chased by a crowd of people up by the main road, therefore this figure, dimly seen through the dark, had to be someone from the lighted house behind him. He came toward Felix rather ineffectually mopping at the blood which was running down his face from the encounter with the baked-bean tin.

'For Gawd's sake get me a drink,' he said in a furious, slurred mutter. 'Get a wiggle on, damn you, my mouth's like the bottom of a birdcage and I've got . . .'

He never revealed what he had got, however. Felix no longer had a can of beans but he had an extremely hard fist. It met Caliban's unshaven chin squarely, almost lifting the older man off his feet, and apart from a grunt as he hit the ground Caliban said nothing further.

Felix ran round to the driver's cab and peered in. The keys were in the ignition. Scarcely thirty seconds later, just as the hunt began to return, disgruntled, Felix drove the Samplex van rather fast out of the yard, round the corner and on to a main road. As the van picked up speed he began to laugh and presently, to sing discordantly. He was free, and very soon he would find a telephone box and ring Summer to make sure that she was safe. Life was exciting and he was one hell of a clever guy!

Felix found a telephone box and after a short sharp word with an operator, rang the cafe. It was late, but one of the girls answered the telephone quite quickly. In answer to his query, however, she gave a worrying reply.

'Summer? Oh, no, I'm afraid you can't speak to her. She went off with her boyfriend ages ago and hasn't come back.'

'Boyfriend? Who's that?'

'Felix Delgado. Who is that speaking, please?'

But Felix, heart thumping, had rung off. The night was no longer starry, his heart no longer sang. He got back into the van again and drove like a demon. He knew he was in Glasgow because he had looked at the telephone directory in the box he had used, and now he must get help for Summer – fast!

The car did not really travel very far, though it seemed a long way to Summer. It stopped on a dark part of the road, by a pine wood. Sanderson drew the vehicle up beneath the sheltering boughs and turned all the lights off, then he came round and opened the back door.

'Come along, my dear, a short walk and then I'll lock you up somewhere for a few hours and tomorrow, when we're far away, you'll be released.' He sounded about as convincing, Summer thought sourly, as a fox addressing a rooster, but she had no chance to tell him this. She mumbled madly through her gag, then subsided into what she hoped he could diagnose as sulky silence. Just let him try anything, that was all! She could still kick!

But in the event, kicking was out of the question, since she had half turned her body towards the door he first opened, and when he sprinted round to the other door she had not managed to get her legs round with her bound wrists impeding her. Sanderson simply dragged her, shoulders first, out of the car.

Summer found her feet and, as he began to bundle her round the back of the vehicle and into the pine wood, also did her damnedest to make his life difficult. She stood stubbornly, refusing to budge, making him drag and pull her every inch of the way, until he was dark-faced and furious. Then he picked her up and staggered a few yards – it was down-hill – but she wriggled and kicked to such good effect that he was forced to drop her once more. They stood nose to nose, glaring, though down Summer's face tears foolishly slid, and down the chemist's, sweat-drops.

'Look, Summer, you're making things difficult for yourself as well as for me. Why won't you come with me? What do you think I'm going to do to you, for God's sake?'

Summer waved her bound wrists and made uncouth noises behind the gag. Sanderson smiled uncertainly.

'You want to be untied? In a moment you shall have your wish. As for the gag, there's no need for it out here. You can shriek like a train and folk won't hear.

Summer made more noises. Sanderson, still holding her arm in a vicelike grip, sighed irritatedly.

'If I take off your gag do you swear you won't

start shrieking? I'm not afraid of you being heard, you must know we're miles from the nearest house, but quite frankly my nerves won't stand much more. If you give me too much trouble I shall put you out.'

Summer nodded fervently, whilst crossing her fingers behind her back. You could tell lies to crooks anyway, she reminded herself, as his fingers fumbled for the bandage, but even so, she did not intend to waste her breath screaming. She had better use for it than that!

'There!' The gag came away and Summer took a deep breath of the fresh night air. 'Now come along, it's down this way.'

Through the trees, Summer could see the glint of moonlit water. Was he going to drown her, hold her under until she died? But if so, why had he taken off the gag? He still had hold of her by the wrists and because it was quite a steep downhill slope, Summer could put up little resistance. I'll save my strength for when we stop, she told herself, but pulled back because it made sense to ensure Sanderson was as weary as possible when she eventually made her break.

They arrived within four feet of the water and Sanderson pushed her down on to the ground. When she tried to move away from him he grabbed her – he was still far from worn out, unfortunately – and then took from his pocket the bottle of whisky.

'Look, my dear, have that little drink I suggested earlier, because presently I'm going to tie your ankles to one of these trees and go off and leave you. You'll be found in the morning, but I don't want you raising the alarm. If you've had enough whisky you'll fall nicely asleep and I shan't have to hit you over your pretty little head or gag you again, which will be nicer for both of us, eh?'

'I'm a tee-totaller,' Summer said madly, through clenched teeth. 'I won't drink it, I won't, you'll have to make me!'

Sanderson stood the bottle down on the ground and turned to her with a sigh, but he looked pleased rather than sorry, Summer saw.

'Then I shall have to . . .'

The opportunity Summer had waited for had arrived. With all her might she kicked out at the whisky bottle and saw it begin to roll quickly, gathering speed as it went, towards the water.

She had known that the whisky bottle was an essential part of whatever vile scheme he had in mind, as soon as he had produced it here. Now she was sure, for he leapt to his feet, cursing, and set off in pursuit of the bottle, obviously completely forgetting that Summer still had her ankles free and plenty of her own particular sort of spirit left.

The moment he moved away Summer was on her feet and scrambling, quick and quiet, up the pine-needled slope. She had gone some way up when she gained the first of the thick bushes which took over as soon as the pine trees were thin enough for other growth to flourish.

'Hey!'

Summer looked briefly back. The chemist was right down by the water and by a miracle, was not even looking in her direction. He was scrabbling with a stick to bring the bobbing whisky bottle nearer to the bank.

Ten seconds later, though, she heard him exclaim again and knew by his tone that she had been missed. Much higher now, and well over to the right of him, she felt a lot safer. She crouched in the deep shadow whilst he cast wildly about, shouting for her, now threatening, now cajoling. He kept reminding her that he had meant well, that she would only have been tied up for a few hours . . . and then, as though he could actually see her, he changed direction and made purposefully for the bushes in which she cowered.

Summer waited until he was almost on her, knowing for the first time the stupid and irrational desire which occasionally strikes all hunted things – the desire to give up. She had to almost physically restrain herself from standing up and saying, 'Here I am,' and watching her captor's despair give way to triumph. But she crouched low and told herself he could not possibly have seen her and sure enough he suddenly turned away, muttering, and set off in the general direction of the car. He must have thought she was making for it and she could imagine now how he must be listening for the first sound of her starting the engine, setting off up the road . . . though how he thought she would steer or change gear or even switch on the ignition with her wrists bound together was beyond her!

She waited until he was right up by the road, and then began, very slowly and carefully, to work her way along the slope, further from him. She wanted to regain the road eventually, but right now all that seemed important was to put as much space as possible between herself and Sanderson. To that effect she continued to move upwards to her right, always moving away from the car.

She stopped moving when she saw, through the striped shadow of the wood, that the chemist had checked the car and was now under the trees once more, standing almost completely still, waiting for her to reveal her whereabouts by a movement. It was scary, but she kept as still as he until, a long, long way off, she heard what sounded at first like an insect's buzz and then resolved itself into a car, coming fast and still in the distance. If only she could get up to the road somehow!

Her mind evolved a plan almost before she knew she was working on it. She waited until the engine sounded more clearly, then with a good deal of difficulty she reached out and took off one of her sneakers. A branch or better still a stone would have been more appropriate, but all she could get at was the shoe. Keeping well down in the shadows and moving with the utmost caution, she awkwardly threw the sneaker as far down the hill as she could hurl it.

It was most satisfactory! The shoe rolled through the undergrowth making quite a good noise and eventually hit the water with a little splash. The chemist, for all his intelligence, rose to Summer's bait like a fish to the fly.

'Got you!' she heard him shout, and then he was blundering downhill so fast that she could see he was in danger of overrunning himself and of landing up as deep in the lake as she was sure he had intended her to be.

The moment he was moving well, Summer got into her crouch again. Up the hill she scurried, keeping low, not daring to look back, and she had very nearly made it to the road when she heard him, far below, give a wild, furious cry.

'Why, you wicked. . . .'

Summer burst out of the trees and lurched into the road just as the car drew level with her. But it was night, and dark, and the driver was concentrating on what lay in the beam of his powerful headlights, not on a small and dirty girl, hands tied, face tear-streaked, who was standing on the verge, with one foot bare, watching his tail-lights grow smaller as he raced past.

Adrenalin had kept Summer going up to thi.
point, making her run uphill with her hands tied
tightly, ignoring her missing sneaker, not even
noticing the cuts and bruises from low-lying branches
and from the harsh, gravelly slope of the hill. Now,
all of a sudden, adrenalin, it seemed, ceased to flow.
Summer stared dully after the car and heard
Sanderson closing noisily in on her with what
amounted to indifference. She knew, vaguely, that
he was a terrified and dangerous man and that she
and she alone stood between him and safety and
respectability. She knew, too, that he had meant to
kill her and that if – when – he caught up with her
now he would probably strangle her with his bare
hands rather than risk losing her again.

But she could go no further, run no more, think
of nothing new. She could only stand, like a dumb
animal, and wait for fate to catch up with her.

She was staring after the car and did not really
notice when the red lights were joined by two white
ones. It had no significance in her exhausted and
numbed mind. Even when the car suddenly,
inexplicably, stopped getting smaller and started
getting bigger she did not notice for several moments
. . . and then she realized. He was reversing! He *had*
seen her, he was coming back . . . But Sanderson had
gained the road and was lurching out of the trees
towards her, his hands held out, his face, when she
turned to look, moulded into a hideous grimace of
hatred and effort.

It galvanized her into action, gave her wings, and
Summer used them. She flew after the car, dot and go
one, and saw, incredulously, that the driver wore a
dark peaked cap and that there was a blue light on
top of the cab, though it was not at the moment
flashing. It was the cops . . . and sitting in the

passenger seat, staring out of the rear window, was Felix!

The car roared to a halt beside her just as Sanderson's hand gripped her shoulder. The driver swung his door open, but someone else was quicker; someone else was out of the car and swinging a clenched fist at Sanderson's unsuspecting chin, Summer realized joyfully. The chemist's fingers mysteriously ceased to grip, went slack, and he fell to the ground with a dull thud, but Summer scarcely noticed. She was too busy being hugged and fussed and made much of by a bright-eyed, beaming Felix Delgado, who could not bring himself to explain where the cavalry had come from or how they had known where she was, so busy was he in making absolutely certain that Summer was all right, that she was not drugged, drowned or dead.

The policemen – for there was another in the back seat – took care of Sanderson whilst Felix cut the tape around Summer's wrists and saw her into the car. He offered to go and look for her sneaker, but Summer waved the suggestion carelessly aside. Why worry about sneakers when she had her life and Felix had his. They had won!

8

'Summer? You awake?'

Summer stirred, tried to burrow deeper beneath the blankets, and felt them twitched away from her face. Light flooded in. Sunlight. Grudgingly, she sat up, blinked, rubbed sleep from her eyes, and saw Felix, with a cup of tea in his hand and an anxious expression on his face which cleared as she smiled at him.

'Thank goodness, I was beginning to wonder if you were all right or whether I ought to get the doctor back.'

The doctor had been summoned at some ungodly hour when they had arrived back at the police station, and he had assured everyone that Summer was a bit cut, bruised and battered and probably too excited to sleep, but that otherwise she was as fit as a fiddle.

'I'll give her a sleeping tablet,' he said heartily, 'and she'll be right as rain in the morning.'

Summer had refused the sleeping pill, however; she had known very well that excitement or not, she would sleep like a log and so she had. She said as much now, taking the cup of tea from Felix and sipping it whilst covertly examining the room which she had been too tired to do when she had got into bed some hours previously.

It was Felix's room, of course. There had been no question of her going back to the cafe, and Felix's landlady proved a pearl beyond price and quite willing to have a young lady sleep in Felix's bed whilst her lodger slept on the living-room couch.

'Like it?'

Summer blushed. Felix knew why she was glancing curiously around her, but having been sussed, she might as well take a good stare.

It was a nice room. It had dark-yellow drapes at the windows, a browny-gold rug on the floor, a very small black-and-white television set on a stand in front of a tiny and probably useless fireplace, and all the usual bits of furniture – a wardrobe, dressing table, chest of drawers and, of course, the bed. There were two pictures on the walls, some photos on the mantelpiece, and a big easy chair filled at the moment with clutter and with Summer's jeans and T-shirt flung casually down on top of Felix's books and papers.

'Umm . . . yes, it's nice. Is that your dog?' Summer pointed to a photo on the mantelpiece. The photo showed a large, shaggy animal with hair hanging all over its eyes standing beside a very pretty, dark-haired girl.

'Sure is. Scruffy, we call him.'

'That's a good name.' Summer drank some more tea. 'Is it too soon to ask what happened to you last night?'

'No, of course not. Where shall I start?'

Summer tried not to let her eyes stray towards the photos on the mantelpiece; it was too bad, why hadn't Felix told her the girl's name as well? Was she someone special? Was she his girlfriend? But he was talking, she must forget about the photos and concentrate.

121

'. . . stopped the van in a little yard, and fortunately for me it was very dark,' Felix was saying. 'I got out, knocking Caliban over in the process, and bolted into hiding. His pals all came out when he yelled but fortunately they all thought I'd run off so of course they followed. I got into the van – he'd left the keys in the ignition – and drove to the nearest police station, which was blocks away, naturally.'

'Gee! And then?'

'Well, I better tell you it properly, not how it happened. It seems your friendly chemist had phoned ahead to Caliban's first delivery to warn them I was aboard, and if he'd gone there my goose would have been cooked, but no one thought about Caliban's own little supply. He simply had to get rid of the drugs he'd stolen before he could go on to the genuine customers; he couldn't risk someone seeing the stuff he'd stashed. So there he was, not at all where he should have been, about to sell his stuff, when I caught him amidships and bowled him over, then drove off in his van. Poor guy!'

'Oh, sure, like poor Sanderson! And then what happened?'

'The police heard me out and to be fair to them, they didn't waste time checking my story or anything like that. They took one look at the "sugar" in the packets I'd got in my pocket, checked with the cafe that you weren't there, and alerted the local cops, which wasn't a lot of good really since they went and grilled Ozzie and Beryl who simply stuck to the story that you'd gone out, presumably with a boyfriend, and no one had seen you since. No one thought of Sanderson, of course, or they might have noticed his car was missing.'

'And you, Felix? How come you were there when I came out of the woods?'

'It was partly luck and partly a hunch, I guess. The luck was that we were tearing back to Castlebridge at that precise minute and the hunch was me, looking back.' Felix was sitting on the end of the bed but now he leaned forward, his dark eyes serious. 'It was weird. We'd gone past you, we hadn't even noticed the car parked right back under the branches. I was concentrating on the road ahead, willing the car to go faster, when I felt such a pull . . . It was almost physical. It brought my head round and I found myself staring out of the rear window, and even then I don't think I actually saw you . . . just a small figure. Something in my head said, "It's Summer!" I yelled to the driver to stop and Christ, his reactions couldn't have been quicker! He stopped and put her in reverse almost in the same movement and I shouted, "Hurry, she's there, by the side of the road!" Then I saw that creep jump you and I was out of the car and swinging at him before you could say knife!'

'So you were. Felix . . .'

'Yes, honey?'

'What *was* Sanderson going to do to me?'

Felix shifted uncomfortably.

'Does it matter? He didn't get round to it, thanks to your cleverness.'

'Yes, I think it does. I . . . I suppose there will be a trial and all sorts. It will have to come out then, won't it?'

'No, I don't think it will. The police will prosecute for the drug business, but they can't do much about attempted murder. They'll just have him for attempted abduction, I suppose.'

'I see. But I want to know. I'd rather.'

'Okay, if that's how you feel. We think he was going to pour whisky into you until you were too drunk to know or care what was going on, and then he was going to throw you in the lake.'

'Drown me, you mean? Yes, I thought that as well.'

'That's it. He thought the authorities would assume you'd gone out with your boyfriend as Sanderson was telling everyone, had a few drinks too many, and fallen in the water and drowned.'

'And what about the boyfriend?'

'Ah well, that was quite clever, really. If the gang had managed to blow me out back in Glasgow, they'd have brought my body back here and dumped me in the water too, perhaps with a turned-over boat to make it look authentic. If they failed, they would have claimed the boyfriend was so scared he'd done a runner. Which isn't all that unlikely, I suppose.'

'And Nell? Did she know what was going on?'

'Sure she did. She and Caliban planned to double-cross the gang and get some of the profit for themselves.'

'And the students? They weren't in on it as well, were they? I seem to remember the chemist saying something about a contact in Marseilles who arranged it all. How was that done?'

'The Drug Squad are on to that and Sergeant Young explained it to me earlier. Apparently the students are all quite genuine and the holiday they book on is genuine enough, too. But the students are all issued with standard-type rucksacks and the blue ones have a secret compartment in the base in which the drug packet is hidden. Beryl knew to search the blue ones – well, not search them because she knew the stuff was there, but how to get it out – and then she handed the raw drug to her uncle, Ned Sanderson, who turned it into an acceptable form in his dispensary, put it into the little sugar packets and returned it to the gift shop. From there, of course, it went to the cafe in the form of supplies for Ozzie's other cafe up in the hills. Caliban picked it up but it never got to the other cafe, it went straight up to Glasgow, to the drug ring, who sold it on the streets to kids not a lot older than you at a huge profit.'

'Gee!' Summer finished her tea and put the mug down on the bedside table, then leaned back luxuriously against her pillows – or rather Felix's pillows, for his landlady had not had a chance to change the bed before her new guest was in it and sleeping soundly! 'It's been a real adventure, hasn't it, Felix? It's been frightening and sickening and so exciting that everything's going to feel mighty flat for a bit!'

'Imagine going home though and telling your Mom and Dad,' Felix said encouragingly. He stood up and picked up Summer's empty cup. 'And then there's your Aunt Peggy . . . Think how amazed she'll be when you go back to her quiet little cottage!'

'Mm hmm,' Summer murmured. 'Yeah, in a few days I'll be having two whole weeks with Aunt Peggy!'

Despite herself she could not sound as enthusiastic as she felt she should. She glanced around the room, away from Felix. If only . . . if only she could stay here, but she had no job any more and no real excuse. Aunt Peggy would be notified as soon as the authorities could get hold of her, that she had a visitor awaiting her return.

'It's Felicity. Her name's Felicity.'

'What? I'm sorry . . .? What do you mean?'

Felix was grinning; he jerked a thumb at the photo on the mantelpiece.

'The girl standing by my dog. Her name's Felicity.'

Summer glanced, with feigned surprise, at the photo on the mantelpiece. 'Who? Oh, *her*. So what?'

'So she's my *sister*, dum-dum! You'd like her.'

A huge smile broke out on Summer's face. She smiled up at Felix with uncomplicated affection. He was real special, was Felix, even when he was at his most irritating.

'She looks nice, and she's awful pretty,' she said. She looked wistfully around the room. What a shame she would only be here for a few more hours. Now that she thought about it, Castlebridge itself was still waiting to be thoroughly explored, to say nothing of the surrounding countryside. She had not taken a boat out on the lake, she had not climbed, she had only been swimming twice . . . and there were other local beauty spots which really should be seen before she made tracks out of here.

'Summer?'

'Mm hmm?'

'You'll be off now, I suppose, to stay with your aunt. Did you know Angela's going to take over the cafe and run it for Ozzie for a bit? He's guilty all right but he's not proven guilty yet. She was telling me this morning she hopes to buy the business once things are settled. She's got plenty of get up and go, has Angela, she'll do okay.'

Summer thought about her aunt's cottage and about a week spent in the company of an elderly English woman. She would be bored out of her mind after the excitement of the past few days and she had friends here, people who knew the *real* Summer, the one who had found out she could do most things if she had to. Why should she go tamely off to her aunt's, when she would enjoy life so much more here, with her friends? She could give her a call, explain . . .

'I guess I'll stay here for a while,' Summer said thoughtfully. 'My aunt'll understand, and Angela could do with me here. I meant to see the sights, get around a bit. Now I'll do it when I'm not needed at the cafe. Felix, what time is it?'

'It's three o'clock. You've missed your lunch.'

'I thought I was hungry! I'd better get up and get going or Angela will take on someone else – say, Felix, if we're neither of us working this afternoon why don't we take one of those boats right up the lake, see what there is to see up there?'

'Swell! Want me to drop in on Angela, explain you'd like to stay on? It won't take long.'

'Yes, if you . . . No, on second thoughts don't explain, just tell her I'll be over in ten minutes. I'll eat there . . . care to join me ? . . . and then see how she feels about keeping me on. She might want to cut down on staff, you can't tell.' Summer looked round the room for her clothes and began to push back the covers.

Felix headed for the door and then, with his hand on it, turned back towards her. He was grinning.

'I'll see Angela and tell her you're on your way over. But don't you realize, Summer, you're a heroine? Guys will come flocking to see the gal who bust a drugs racket!' He sketched a salute and left the room whilst behind him Summer laughed and jumped out of bed.

She was looking around for her sneakers, with her cut-offs and T-shirt already donned, when she remembered where her second sneaker was – probably in several metres of water. Shrugging, she headed for the stairs. Once, she would have felt a real schmuck going into a cafe with only one shoe, but now she knew details like that were unimportant. She could go up to her room and get sandals or something when she'd had her talk to Angela. Then she really must ring Mom collect and break it to her that she wanted to stay here until vacation was over, hint that she'd met a dreamy guy . . . She would call Pop too, and tell him all the details that would upset Mom, all the dangerous, dreadful things which had happened, because Pop would understand and see that he'd done right to send her to England. Felix had been joshing when he'd called her a heroine, but her time in the Lakes had taught her a lot. I'm as good as anyone, any day, Summer told herself exultantly. I asked Felix for a date – as good as – and he said 'Swell' without a second thought!

Singing beneath her breath, Summer padded down the stairs to start her new life.

THE END